The ART Of ARCHITECTURAL DRAWING

Imagination and Technique

THOMAS WELLS SCHALLER AIA

VAN NOSTRAND REINHOLD

I(T)P® A Division of International Thomson Publishing Inc.

New York • Albany • Bonn • Boston • Detroit • London • Madrid • Melbourne
Mexico City • Paris • San Francisco • Singapore • Tokyo • Toronto

Cover design: Paul Costello
Cover Illustrations: Thomas W. Schaller

Van Nostrand Reinhold Staff:
    Executive Editor: Roberto de Alba
    Editor: Jane Degenhardt
    Production Editor: Carla M. Nessler
    Production Manager: Mary McCartney
    Designer: Nancy Freeborn

Copyright © 1997 by **Van Nostrand Reinhold**

I(T)P® A division of International Thomson Publishing Inc.
The ITP logo is a registered trademark under license.

Printed in the United States of America

For more information, contact:

Van Nostrand Reinhold
115 Fifth Avenue
New York, NY 10003

Chapman & Hall GmbH
Pappelalle 3
69469 Weinheim, Germany

Chapman & Hall
2-6 Boundary Row
London SE1 8HN
United Kingdom

International Thomson Publishing Asia
221 Henderson Road #05-10
Henderson Building
Singapore 0315

Thomas Nelson Australia
102 Dodds Street
South Melbourne, 3205
Victoria, Australia

International Thomson Publishing Japan
Hirakawacho Kyowa Building, 3F
2-2-1 Hirakawacho
Chiyoda-ku, 102 Tokyo
Japan

Nelson Canada
1120 Birchmount Road
Scarborough, Ontario
Canada M1K 5G4

International Thomson Editores
Seneca 53
Col. Polanco
11560 Mexico D.F. Mexico

1 2 3 4 5 6 7 8 9 10   RRD-CW   03 02 01 00 99 98 97

Library of Congress Cataloging-in-Publication Data

Schaller, Thomas W. (Thomas Wells). 1950-
    The art of architectural drawing : imagination and technique / Thomas Wells Schaller.
        p. cm.
    Includes bibliographical references and index.
    ISBN 0-442-00993-3
    1. Architectural rendering—Technique. I. Title.
720'.28—dc20   95-45733
                                         CIP

http:/www.vnr.com
product discounts • free email newsletters
software demos • online resources
email: info@vnr.com
A service of I(T)P®

FOR NANCY

"If nothing else, the years have taught me this: if there's a pencil in your pocket, there's a good chance that one day you'll feel tempted to start using it."

—PAUL AUSTER

Figure D–1. *Proposed Cliff Structure, China.* (1996) **T.W. Schaller.** Watercolor and pencil, 70.2cm x 31.2cm

CONTENTS

FOREWORD

by Paul Rudolph

The architectural drawing is the most eloquent tool a professional has to communicate design ideas. Its subject may vary from a city to a small detail but its objective is always to inform the act of building. As a practical tool, drawing allows the architect to explore a great variety of schemes—adding, subtracting, and rearranging elements, materials, and systems before reaching a final design solution. As a conceptual tool, it indulges the architect in exploring the ideal worlds of the imagination.

The freehand sketch and the measured drawing or rendering have been, for centuries, the most traditional forms of architectural drawing. Today, the computer drawing is well on its way to challenging the traditional drawing. This, to a degree, is a generational preference. But we must be aware that the techniques utilized in developing an architectural idea profoundly influence the design results.

The freehand sketch is a record of the design process throughout the length of a project. It is a private document often comprehensible only to its creator, embodying the pure essence of the effort involved in making it. To some degree the sketch is the guardian of the design, protecting the integrity of the architectural idea and warning the architect when extraneous or inappropriate elements begin to creep into the composition.

For an architect, sketching is often an exhilarating exploration, a crescendo, that leads to a sort of ecstasy as it approaches "the moment of truth" when architectural balance is achieved. The sketch often reveals the working of the inner mind in unique ways that cannot be duplicated by any other means. It has its own inner logic, and when used often enough it can become a trusted guide towards true invention. In his *Codex Leicester,* Leonardo Da Vinci gives us a marvelous example of thought translated into drawing, and illustrates the fact that the creative process takes a great deal of time and is often the prelude to superior artistic achievement.

The rendering, or measured drawing, seeks to express what its subject—city, building, or object—looks like, and has the unique capacity to convey multiple scales simultaneously (something a model can seldom accomplish). One of its great advantages is that it conveys actual dimensions, the reason why renderings are sometimes used to inform the design process, much as sketches are. One of its most obvious limitations is that it usually represents a somewhat ideal, single point of view. But it is a point of view that most people understand, and that is why renderings are most often used as sales tools—by the architect to sell his idea to the client, or by the client to sell his project to others. Therefore renderings are inevitably idealized and often "made pretty" to be more effective sales tools.

As we can see in the striking examples presented in this book,
the architectural drawing is a powerful visual-communications tool, and still today, the most effective vehicle to convey the essence of the art of building.

PREFACE

Just as the term "architecture" can be applied to discussions of a specific building, buildings in general, or the act of designing buildings in the first place, the phrase "architectural drawing" can have several meanings as well. Visual representations of architecture can be used to envision and design a specific building, and to document or clarify the construction specifics of a structure to be built. In addition, architectural drawings may be used to portray or interpret the essence of particular structures for design proposals, competitions, or marketing purposes. Finally, architectural artwork can be used to record, or even to dream of, ideas about buildings or architecture and its influence. These types of works may be either building or non-building specific and may in fact more rightly be called examples of fine art in which the process and the elements of architectural design, both known and imagined, are used as

Figure P–1. *Tower of Babel.* (1563) **Pieter Breugel the Elder (1525/30–1569).** Oil on wood, Kunsthistorisches Museum, Vienna.

The "Myth of Babel" is represented here in an equally powerful allegorical work of art by the great Netherlandish master. An atypically biblical and "architectural" work for the humanist landscape painter, it resonates to this day with the idea of the supreme folly of man's earthly ambition.

subject matter—inspiration. Clearly, these first types of drawings or paintings are about building, the tangible art of architecture, while the latter are more concerned with the intangible, ideas about building perhaps, but more about art itself.

The focus of this book is not building, but the images that both derive from and inspire the act of building. Moreover, a special emphasis is placed upon those works of art that do not have any existent material body, a "real building," as their aim. The discussion is in no way meant to be construed as qualitative in nature; all the pursuits, the types of drawing thus far defined, have an individual as well as a collective value and purpose. In fact, it can be argued that one type could not fully exist with the other types. The field of architectural drawing is, as a whole, too often seen simply as an adjunct, a by-product, of architectural design—an "art about an art." It is the sincere aim of this book to demonstrate not only the interdependence of these disciplines, but the viability of the various forms of architectural representation as distinct from the art of architectural building. Each discipline nourishes and

Figure P–2. *Tokyo City Hall Competition; Computer-Generated Interior Perspective View of Atrium.* (1988) **Artist/Designer: Arata Isosaki.** Ink jet print on paper from the office of Arc Yamagiwa, Tokyo, 76.8cm x 108.6cm; Courtesy of Centre d'Architecture Canadien/Canadian Centre for Architecture, Montreal.

Known primarily for the large scale silk-screen representations of his designs—typically seen in plan and elevation—which are a modernist take on Beaux-Arts graphics, this somewhat unusual three-point perspective is a convincing alternative and a highly effective way of organizing the visual elements of this interior space.

informs the other; each, if it would not fail completely, would exist in a far more meager state if not for the other.

In the pages to follow, the essential difference between the acts of building-making and image-making will be discussed, and the very genesis of image-making itself—what we see and the way we see it through the use of architectural images—will be looked upon. Also to be explored is how architectural images are composed, the choice of media and graphic devices which effect the best or most appropriately described result. Various forms of architectural graphic communication—how these various drawing types differ from each other and why one may be seen as more appropriate at times than another—will be examined next. Examples, both historic and contemporary, of work from some of the world's most outstanding architects and architectural artists are included to demonstrate principles of design and design communication—mass, volume and space, gesture, movement, content and intent, as well as shade and shadow, intonation, color, and atmosphere. Finally, examples of

Figure P–3. *Fantastic Monuments.* (CA.1747–1750) **Giovanni Battista Piranesi (1720–1778).** Pen, brown ink, and brown wash over graphite on cream laid paper, 19.8cm x 27.7cm; Courtesy of Centre d'Architecture Canadien/Canadian Centre for Architecture, Montreal.

The actual genesis of this piece is speculative; there are representative elements of the *Prima Parte* from 1743, though this work was completed some years later. The full range of visionary architectural elements, theatrical use of lighting effects, and bold compositional imagery mark this as an example of the artist's more developed style.

Figure P–4. *Studio di l'Architeture Assassinee.* (1974) **Aldo Rossi.** Ink, 21cm x 29.7cm

Far more than an academic, isolated mind is at work here in this witty, expressive, and personal "architectural" assemblage with its implicit dialogue on the conflict of chaos and order.

more abstract, non-building directed idea representation are included. Design investigation, architectural fantasies, and dreams are the emphasis here. An attempt will be made to explore the answer or answers to the question of how these types of artworks derive from or even inspire eventual design. Moreover, emphasis will be made upon what these purely image-based efforts have to say about the relationship of architecture and humankind. Are our buildings and our cities a reflection of our civilization or are our civilizations and behavior at least in part reflections of our built environment?

Figure P–5. *Proposed Stage Set, "Death in Venice."* (1991) **T.W. Schaller.** Watercolor, 46cm x 46cm

A simple stair and a mysterious light set the atmosphere and reveal the essential idea of this piece which seeks to layer and obscure information and to defer resolution for a heightened sense of the unknown.

As a final note, it is hoped that the reader will discover in the words and images represented herein that the would-be designer or architect, seeking to build a better, more useful, or more beautiful world could only be exceptionally well-served by the decision to "think with a pencil"—to investigate his or her ideas by means of visual representation. To clarify, that investigation should be equally valid and fruitful whether that "pencil" might assume the form of a pen, a brush, and even a computer screen. Better, that is to say more informed drawing, can lead only to better, more informed buildings. And lastly, the book attempts to demonstrate the viability, power, and beauty of architectural artwork, not as a means to one end, or necessarily even as an end itself, but as emblematic of the larger process of creative thinking. It is this process that is the real focus, not any one drawing or painting or building. "It is art," wrote Henry James, "that makes life . . . and I know of no substitute whatever for the force and beauty of its process."

ACKNOWLEDGMENTS

The author wishes to express his sincere gratitude to the following groups and individuals without whose dedication, efforts, and generosity, this book would not have been possible:

The Graham Foundation for much appreciated support and a belief in the project.

The design, production, and editorial staffs of Van Nostrand Reinhold who, over the years, have proven their belief in architectural artwork many times over; and especially to Roberto de Alba, Beth Harrison, Jane Degenhardt, Paul Costello, Nancy Freeborn, Mary McCartney, and Carla Nessler. A special word of thanks to John Griffin and Wendy Lochner for keeping the project alive.

Mr. Paul Rudolph for his generosity, well-considered text, and a legacy of images.

Mr. Gavin Stamp of the Macintosh School of Architecture in Glasgow for his scholarship, assistance, and continued support.

The numerous institutions around the world who kindly permitted the reproduction of images from their respective collections: The Avery Architectural and Fine Arts Library, Columbia University, in the City of New York; The New York Historical Society; The Smithsonian Institution's National Museum of Design, New York; The Pierpont Morgan Library, New York; The Art Institute of Chicago; The National Gallery of Art, Washington D.C.; The Toledo Museum of Art, Toledo, Ohio; The Frank Lloyd Wright Archives, Taliesen West, Scottsdale, Arizona; The Minneapolis Institute of Arts, Minnesota; The Ames Gallery, Berkeley, California; Centre D'Architecture Canadien, Montreal; Kunsthistorisches Museum, Vienna; Cordan Art, Baarn, Holland; Nationalgalerie, Staatliche museen du Berlin; École Nationale des Beaux Arts, Paris; Bibliotèque Nationale de France, Paris; Metropolitan Cathedral of Christ the King, Liverpool; The British Architectural Library, The Royal Institute of British Architects, London; Sir John Soane's Museum, London; and Her Majesty, Queen Elizabeth II, The Royal Collection, Windsor.

The many skilled draftsmen and studio assistants who, over the years, have played no small part in the production of many of the images created by the author's studio and represented in this book: Andrew Fitzsimmons, Moritoshi Nakamura, Vladislav Yeliseyev, Janek Konarski, Tom Murphy, Roger Lee, and especially, Mr. Robert Becker.

Ms. Eliza Beckwith for typing and administrative skills, support, and friendship.

Ms. Bonnie Grossman, Ms. Sally Forbes, and Mr. David Garrard Lowe, as well as the memberships of The American Society of Architectural Perspectivists, The New York Society of Renderers, the Japanese Architectural Renderers Association, the Korean Architectural Perspectivists Association, the Society of Architectural and Industrial Illustrators of Great Britain, and the Lawrence Institute of Technology for their individual and collective efforts in advancing the cause of architectural artwork worldwide.

Elizabeth Day, Joyce Rosner, Doug Jamieson, Curtis Woodhouse, and Gordon Grice for being there. Cathie, Erin, Sarah, Nathan, Adam, Ben, and Tommy for their talents, and the rest of my family and friends for patience and understanding.

And finally, the great number of artists and architects—colleagues, clients, and friends—whose unforgettable visions are represented herein and whose skills and generosity have made this a far richer volume.

PART ONE

EVOLUTION
of
TECHNIQUE

House. (1956) **T.W. Schaller.** Ink and crayon, 30cm x 23cm

The Odyssey Project. (1996) **T.W. Schaller. Architects: Frank Lloyd Wright and others.** Watercolor, 117cm x 58.5cm; Courtesy of The Otis Elevator Company.

Due to the sheer physical size of this proposed design and in order to maximize visual impact, the rendering of specific detail was avoided in favor of sculptural form. In addition and toward the same end, the light, cool tones of the focus structure contrast with the darker, warmer treatment of sky and overall atmosphere.

Ameritrust Tower. (1991) **T.W. Schaller. Architects: Kohn Pedersen Fox.** Watercolor and pencil, 70.2cm x 42.9cm

The essential design gesture created by the juxtaposition of a solid masonry tower and a floating glass plane is treated graphically as a simple dialogue between warm and cool tonalities.

(left) La Défense Competition, Paris, France. (1995) **T.W. Schaller. Architects: Cesar Pelli and Associates.** Watercolor and pencil, 42.9cm x 66.3cm

This vigorous graphic treatment demonstrates that it is entirely possible to describe an evolving architectural presence by an emphasis upon volume, light, and context rather than by design specificity.

(below) Proposed Development, Newport Beach, California, park view. (1994) **T.W. Schaller. Architects: Aldo Rossi, Studio di Architettura.** Watercolor, 70.2cm x 93.6cm

Color is as deeply important to this image as it was to the development of the design scheme it seeks to interpret.

(left) South Pointe Development Competition. (1993) **Curtis James Woodhouse. Architects: Arquitectonica with STA and the Portofino Group.** Watercolor, 35cm x 31cm

(below) Resort Hotel Proposal, Portugal. (1991) **T.W. Schaller. Architects: Arquitectonica.** Watercolor, 28cm x 43cm

As designer, Bernardo Fort-Brescia of Arquitectonica sought a highly charged sense of vitality and informality for the multifarious forms of these proposals. The graphics, therefore, needed to be as varied and lively in color range and composition to effectively tell the story.

Baltimore Performing Arts Center Competition. (1994) **Artist/Designer: Rafael Vignoly.** Charcoal and color pencil

This compelling and vigorous image records an instantaneous design impulse; a few brisk lines and tones—the cool blue of the superstructure above and the deep black of the earth below—establish the essential information clearly and concisely. This is a designer who truly "thinks with a pencil."

Baltimore Performing Arts Center Competition. (1994)
T.W. Schaller. Architects: Lett/Smith, Toronto.
Watercolor and pencil, 51cm x 76cm overall

This composite of gestural vignettes establishes an effective and atmospheric progressive "walk-through" of this large design concept proposal by the well-considered choices of view.

Chinese Grain Infrastructure—Export Terminal, China. (1993) **Barbara Worth Ratner. Architects: Simons-Eastern.** Watercolor and color pencil, 101.4cm x 78cm

This image of a generic terminal "was created to elicit interest in developing a comprehensive system of terminals with rail and water links" for the distribution of goods within China. "The red of the sky was selected for its association with joy and prosperity," and it is in perfect sync with the simple bold forms of the design.

Puebla New Town, Puebla, Mexico. **Steve Parker. Architects: Hellmuth, Obata & Kassabaum.** Watercolor, 31.2cm x 24.38cm

The bold palette and free watercolor treatment of this early design phase sketch could not be more appropriate to the subject matter, to its intended usage, and to the selected site.

The Four Continents Bridge, Hiroshima, Japan. (1988) **Artist/Designer: James Wines, SITE.**

This image, completed as a design proposal for the Hiroshima Sea and Island Expo in 1989, is another investigation of the bridge form as destination. The structure symbolizes the connections between land, sea, and people. In order to establish a valuable link of respect and responsibility, the insinuating elements of all three of these influences extend across the span in unison.

III–9. (1995) **Artist/Designer: Willem van den Hoed.** Watercolor, 10.2cm x 15.3cm

Architect/artist Williem van den Hoed continues his sketchbook-based architectonic explorations by, in this case, adding an amorphous shape with geometrical voids subtracted from it to a rectilinear baseform. Using colors along the warm-to-cool spectrum establishes a strong dialogue.

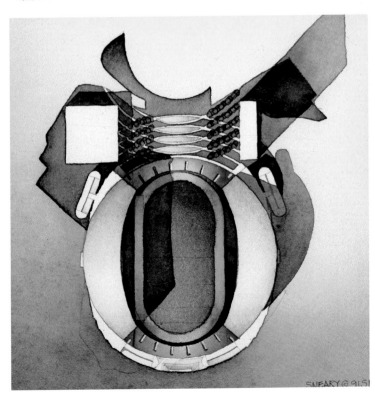

Hong Kong Soccer Stadium. **Richard Sneary (and Susan Lynn). Architects: Hellmuth Obata and Kassabaum Sports Facilities Group, Kansas City, MO.** Watercolor, 17.9cm x 17.9cm

A deeply effective image on several levels, this work succeeds in imparting clear information about the structural proposal in its eventual three dimensions and acts as a singularly successful work of art.

Untitled. (1976) **Aldo Rossi.** Ink and markers, 20cm x 30cm

The choice of strong complementary tones of red and green, used here establish a clear dialogue between the horizontal and vertical forces of the image, creates a subsequent architectural identity.

Forest House. (1996) **Artist/Designer: Samuel Ringman.** Watercolor, 23.4cm x 23.4cm

Ringman is an architect/artist who explores, via the graphic image, "nature as an integral part of architecture." Of this view, he writes, "the emergence of the building from the rock outcropping and the regeneration of plants on the structure reinforce the concept of the house as an integral part of the forest, not as an object placed within it."

Cascade House. (1996) **Artist/Designer: Samuel Ringman.** Watercolor, 23.4cm x 23.4cm

The sentiment of this image reminds one of Piranesi and of Cole's historical preoccupations. Of the house, Ringman writes, it "is integrated into an extraordinary site at its most dramatic point; appearing as a barricade, it actually leaves the stream's flow uninterrupted. The house is a juxtaposition of natural and ordered elements, contrasting man's built environment with the natural forces that will erode and reclaim it."

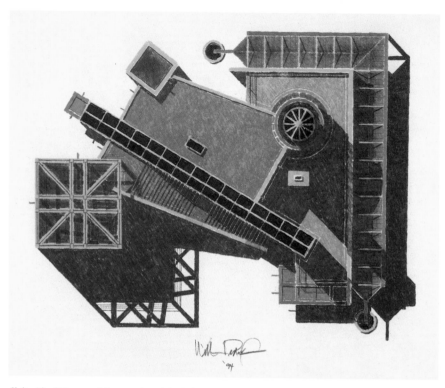

Shelter Island House, roof plan view. (1994) **Artist/Designer: William Pedersen FAIA.** Prismacolor pencil, 46cm x 46cm

One of the principal framers of modern skyscraper identity, William Pedersen displays some of the fundamentals of his design impetus in a simple rendered plan view. A bold composition of simple forms creates one of the primary themes discerned in his much larger-scale buildings—strong axial motifs, harmony and discord, balance and asymmetry, conflict and resolution. In its clarity and directness, this image possesses the strength of abstract art.

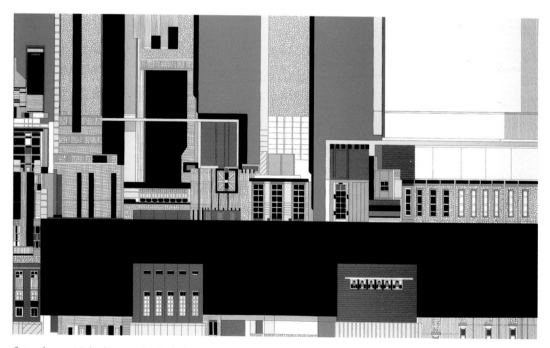

Serigraph:9202. **Michael Insetta.** Limited edition private benefit print, 56.4cm x 33.3cm; Printer: Jon Cone Editions, East Topsham, Vermont. Collection: Michael Insetta

Architectural language is abstracted here in both formal and expressive terms to create this striking work of art, which echoes Bauhaus and Constructivist aesthetic as well as DeStijl and the subsequent reductivist paintings of Mondrian.

Hayden Planetarium, American Museum of Natural History, New York City. (1995) **John E. Fernandez. Architects: J.S. Polshek and Partners.** Watercolor

This versatile architect/artist continues to effectively explore design by means of the informal perspective study sketch. In this case, a particularly sculptural interior space is revealed very successfully.

Hancock/Axial I, Boston. (1995) **Frank M. Costantino.** Watercolor, 24.3cm x 35.8cm

This unique image takes a creative and visionary look at an existing structure—Pei's famous Hancock tower in Boston. While attempting to maintain and respect its iconography, the designer/artist (one of the premier architectural visualists of our day) has graphically suggested changes to the form of the building to add scale, texture, and a more emphatic street wall axis. The well-considered choice of viewpoint and atmospheric condition result in most effective story telling.

South Orange County Regional Civic Center, California. (1992) **Elizabeth Ann Day. Architects: Albert C. Martin with Vitetta Group.** Watercolor, 101.4cm x 74.1cm

Information through color usage is as much the essential idea of this work as is any structural form; thus, the warm roof tones frame primary spaces and axes. The composite of several views adds focus and enhances the overall narrative success.

China Airport. **Georgeanne Deen. Architect: Kanner Associates.** Gouache, 17cm x 25cm

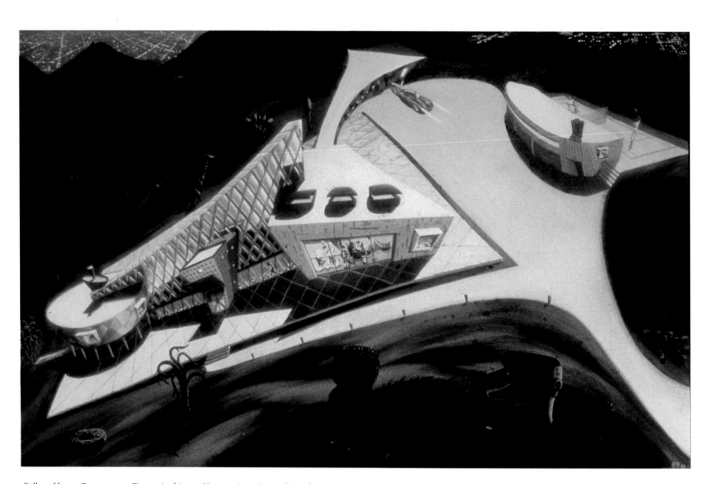

Pollyea House. **Georgeanne Deen. Architect: Kanner Associates.** Gouache, 20cm x 30cm

The landscape and urban-allegory paintings from the 1930s of American Thomas Hart Benton (to say nothing of numerous more modern pop culture references!) echo through the work of this unique artist. By unusual composition and use of skewed perspective, Los Angeles-based artist Georgeanne Deen captures the exuberant intent of the design architects in a witty and entirely appropriate manner.

CHAPTER ONE

A Drawing Is Not a Building

Buckminster Fuller, hero and venerable father figure to many a would-be modern day Renaissance man or woman, was fond of regaling audiences of his books and lectures with the fact that he was born with crossed eyes. The condition was eventually corrected with glasses years later after he had developed a life-long practice of seeing the world around him only in large shapes, shades of light and dark, or "pattern clues," to borrow his phrase. In Fuller's case, this obstacle was transformed by effort and innate gifts into the unique ability to see things—objects, conditions, patterns of behavior, and perhaps even people and ideas—not simply for what they appeared to be at the moment but for what *potential* they

Figure 1–1. *Compositional Invention of Diverse Volumes with Decorative Coloring.* (1933) **Artist/Designer: Iakov Georgievich Chernikov (1889–1951).** Color lithograph (lithographer unknown), 24.0cm x 35.4cm; Courtesy of Centre d'Architecture Canadien/Canadian Centre for Architecture, Montreal.

One of the most prolific and influential protagonists of the Russian Constructivist movement, Chernikov produced some 17,000 drawings of imaginary designs and in excess of fifty books of architectural theory and graphics. He firmly believed in the necessity of architectural graphic representation in mankind's attempt to effectively shape the future.

might possess. His passion was for the *concept* over the *particular*. This "big picture" approach—proceeding from the general to the specific—can be seen as a hallmark of any successful artform—architectural artwork no less so than painting, music, literature, or architecture itself. This "clarity of concept" precedes, even dictates, the refinement of detail.

As architectural image-making is the focus of this work, it is important to attempt to comprehend what value this form of endeavor may have within the overall fields of both image-making and architecture as a whole. That architecture is or can be a form of art is seldom disputed, but some understanding of its place in the overall spectrum of artistic expression is also needed. The philosopher Havelock Ellis considered architecture, the art of building, as the genesis, or starting point, of all the arts that "lie outside the person." Its aim is object-oriented, yet unlike sculpture, the architectural object must almost always have a use—a function. Similarly, the philosophical idealist Hegel dubbed architecture the most primal of all the true arts in its ability to act as both "place" and "symbol"—separate but necessary functions in the attempt to create something that can, in the words of Goethe, "link souls together." It is obvious enough that architecture can act as a place for the collective experience that can, it is hoped, uplift, inspire, and thereby connect one human spirit to another. However, what it may symbolize is another question altogether. To form an answer, it is critical to differentiate between the various meanings of the word "architecture." It can, for instance, refer to either a specific building, buildings in general, or more inclusively, the act of studying or executing the design of buildings. These are related but very

Figure 1–2. *Proposed Corporate Headquarters, Armonk, New York.* (1995) **T.W. Schaller. Architects: Kohn Pedersen Fox.** Watercolor and pencil, 42.9cm x 66.3cm

A slightly distant and decidedly horizontal visual treatment of this schematic design was chosen to contrast with the verticality and emphasize the calm of the heavily wooded earth-bound site.

different endeavors; each has different possibilities. One building may symbolize something quite different than another building—consider the differences between a church and a bank, for example. Similarly, a drawing of a church or a bank as representative of both the proposed structures and the act of designing it may act as another sort of symbol.

The distinction between the art of architecture as *object*, a completed building, and the art of architecture as *process*, the act of design, is crucial for any discussion of architectural artwork. Painting, drawing, computer graphics, and image-making in general are largely about the artistic process; whereas a completed building, even a building widely perceived as a great work of art, can only *represent* the artistic process. The *idea* may manifest but the image or representation of ideas, as it is being perceived by the viewer—is a process in itself. Any student of art or western philosophy knows the indispensability of the concept of process in art-making—painting, music, architecture, or for that matter, the art of living. It is the doing, physical or intellectual, that validates what has been or what may yet be done.

Figure 1–3. *Compact Disc Cover, The Four Nation's Ensemble.* (1992) **T.W. Schaller.** Watercolor, 25cm x 25cm
The attempt of a lyrical "Piranesian" conceit was most communicative of the tone of the early Romantic compositions of the musical program.

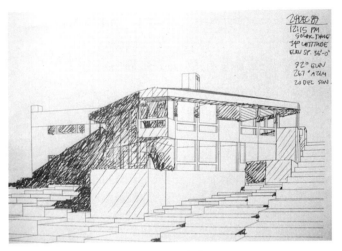

Pencil and Computer Image, Sun Angle Calculations.

Architron Model.

Site Masking.

Photo Montage.

Figure 1–4. *Ojo de Dios, Taos, New Mexico.* (1988–1996) **Artist/Designer: Paul Stevenson Oles FAIA.** Various media.

An on-going project for an eventual family "Taos Haos," the plan impetus for this design came from a Mexican Huichol Indian tradition. Upon the birth of a child, a father would begin weaving in yarn on a cross of sticks, an "Ojo de Dios" (god's eye), as a charm to ward off evil. A harmonius blend of hand-done and computer imagery combine in both the planning and presentation of this design by one of the master visualists of our day.

It is collective knowledge about the evolution of *doing* that represents progress for a society or an individual. Striving toward the *Absolute* virtually defines what most of us in our individual ways have come to know as art.

Sartre, the existential subjectivist, defined man as "nothing but what he may make of himself." This anti-determinist view is at odds with the writings of other philosophical minds, but not to the extent that most would deny that it is the *process* of living that in many ways forms, quite literally, the parameters of our lives. Eighteenth century idealist R.H. Bradley defined sentient experience as the only true reality. A house, for instance, cannot exist for us without our having a clear idea of what a house may be. If the mind cannot know it, in Bradley's world, it cannot be real. If to grasp an idea is what makes it real for us, then the more ideas one can know, the more real life becomes. This defined the process of living for Bradley, a process which, by design, is a march toward the Absolute. For some, the concept of the Absolute can mean complete knowledge, perfection, ideal love, beauty, or God; for the romantically morbid though, it can mean even death or oblivion.

Considerations of religious belief notwithstanding, many thinkers have found a correlation between the concept of the Infinite and that of the human struggle as represented or expressed by the artistic endeavor or process. Thomas Aquinas noted the "claritas" of pure art "a luminous silent stasis of aesthetic pleasure." Joyce, too, termed the highest art—finite beauty—as static, suspended in space, or ultimately, as death. These men were discussing the Absolute, the destination, the purpose of process—what gives mankind its definition, its reason for being, its greatest joy, and its deepest sorrow. For them and many other creative minds, it is this process, this struggle toward perfection and a destination, which, as it is

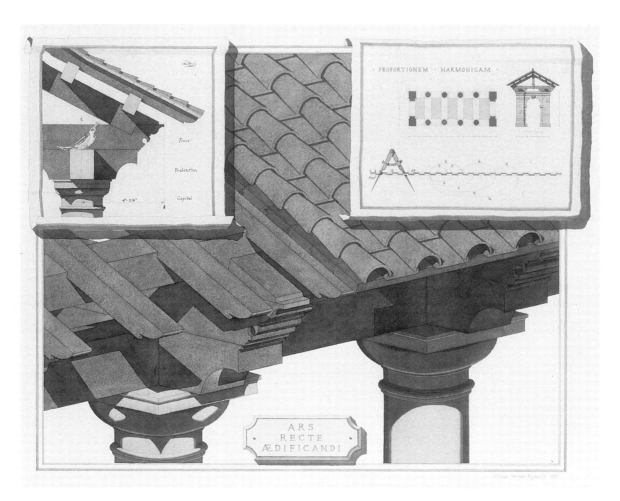

Figure 1–5. *Ars Recte Aedifscandi.* (CA. 1990) **Artist/Designer: Thomas Norman Rajkovich.** Watercolor and ink wash, 51.2cm x 61.5cm

"In his *De Re Aedificatoria*," writes Rajkovich, "the fifteenth-century architect and theorist Leon Battista Alberti describes the fundamental compositional elements of architecture: column and beam (trabeation), wall and arch, and roof. This proposal for a market loggia is designed as a study in the combination of those elements as they recall the tectonic origins of classical architecture."

Figure 1–6. *Civitas Navigabilis.* (CA. 1990) **Artist/Designer: Thomas Norman Rajkovich.** Watercolor and ink wash, 92.3cm x 117.9cm

Of his rich urban invention, modern classicist Rajkovich writes, "A true renaissance of the classical city today requires an understanding of the critical symbolic and perspectival relationships which buildings and monuments form with one another . . . This drawing is intended as an idealized demonstration of what is possible; that the observer might aspire to comprehend, construct, and inhabit Paradise."

understood shall never be reached, that has art as its expressive core. The more static the art, the more distant and abstract it becomes, the closer to infinity and perfection. By contrast, the more kinetic the artform, the more real, lifelike, and process-oriented it is. Along this spectrum, the form of art that is most real or beautiful is a far too complex and subjective discussion for this book. However architecture, at least as it is represented by the acts of designing and building in the view of Ellis, Hegel, and Victor Hugo, who termed it the "great mother-art," can be seen as the most "human," kinetic, active, and process-oriented of all artforms.

The emphasis here upon process is meant to clarify the differences between architecture as structure, architecture as the act of design, which has a structure as its aim, and finally, the creation of architectural artwork, which may not have anything to do with the creation of any particular building at all. It is the latter of these two with which this book is most deeply concerned. These later types of drawing and painting at times seek to represent actual buildings, but more to the point, attempt to visually represent *ideas* about buildings—actual or not—in an effort to document the process of idea development.

"The more any building as idea is true to the idea itself," states Frank Lloyd Wright in *A Testament*, "the better I like the building." While it may be true that in the realm of architecture only a building can actually *be* an idea, only a drawing can document the process of that idea's genesis or evolution. When the idea concerns an architectural concept that may not or cannot as of yet, if ever, come to fruition as a built reality, then there is no more proper venue for its documentation than the field of architectural art. It cannot be said that Wright could be considered, even remotely, a "paper architect"; his legacy of built structures is astonishing. Yet no less prolific or meaningful was the stream of unbuilt and possibly unbuildable projects that flowed from his pen onto the two dimensions of a sheet of paper. It is not likely, for instance, that he believed his famous mile-high building planned for Chicago was ever destined to see the light of day. This fact did not stop his drawing, his dreaming of it, or his assertions that it was indeed buildable. In fact, it was not only Wright's most impressive track record of built structures, but his inveterate habit of "dreaming on paper" that eventually caused so many of the frontiers of design and construction practice to be explored and expanded forever. Bradley agreed that if you could not know it, it could not be, while Kant believed that things we don't know can exist even if we cannot imagine them. Wright was one who could both imagine "unreal" things and, more often than not, make them real.

The distinction between architectural ideas as drawn and those as built should not be dismissed. The value of the graphic abilities of an architect who draws as well as a professional architectural illustrator is lost within a greater discussion of architecture and is thereby overshadowed by it. When an architect produces design concept sketches or construction documents for a proposed building, this work, no matter how beautiful it may be, should rightly be considered as being in service to the structure that may result. The same can be said of the efforts of a commercial illustrator or architectural perspectivist who may be asked to produce presentation drawings for the same building. However, when an architect, artist, or perspectivist "dreams on paper" using the vocabulary of design or even less well-defined architectural concepts such as *inspiration*, the resultant artwork may have merit not unlike any other form of artistic expression and merit beyond the confines of known architectural practice.

One of the aims of this book is to clarify and showcase differing forms of architectural graphics. Moreover, an attempt has been made to illuminate the appropriateness of their various applications in the fields of architecture, architectural investigation, and fine art. Any implied or actual comparison between types of architectural graphics or indeed between any form of architectural artwork and architecture is not qualitative by intent. On the contrary, it is hoped that this book will help to clarify both the interdependence as well as the independence of each of these disciplines. It is not so much the question that one

I

II

III

IV

Figure 1–7. *Aerie.* (1995) **Artist/Designer: Samuel Ringman.** Watercolor, each: 15.3cm x 15.3cm

Of this exploratative design development series, Ringman writes, "A house is framed against the sky to dramatize its ability to respond to the ever-changing conditions of season and climate." The framework of the house is a structural grid upon which panels of glass or solid material can be moved at the discretion of the occupants or the dictates of weather.

could exist without the other but how well it might exist. Of course, a drawing or a painting of a building is not a building, but neither is a building a drawing or a painting. And so, while the ideas and elements of design may result in a better drawing or painting, an inventive and imaginative vision may eventually result in a better building. It stands to reason that the aspiring architect who "thinks with a pencil" may have a greater opportunity to produce a valid work of art than one who does not.

Figure 1–8. *Proposed Performing Arts Center, London.* (1992) **T.W. Schaller.** Watercolor, 56cm x 56cm
An intentionally "claustrophobic" composition was selected for this work to emphasize the constraint imposed by the design response to a dense, urban site.

There are architects who effectively design or study characteristics of a building using non-graphic methods; specifically, the architectural model. While it cannot be said that this practice is wrong, the three-dimensional miniature is, by its very nature, limited to and abstracted by its tangibility. The architectural model is unsurpassed at demonstrating specifics of form but it can cause difficulty in affording the viewer a full understanding of a proposed building's contextuality at least in its more intimate, human-scale aspects. Issues of mass, perspective, and scale notwithstanding, only by means of the drawing can one abstract or isolate the *essential idea* sufficiently in an attempt to ascertain not only the proposed building's physical character, but its full contextual spirit, the feeling it may eventually inspire in the viewer. This expressed duality, the synthesis of the physical and the spiritual, the objective and the subjective, is what the preeminent architectural artist of our century, Hugh Ferriss, termed the "entire truth" about architecture and that which he felt not only necessary, but incumbent upon architectural artists as well as architects, to attempt to capture in their work.

A further defense of the notion of the viability of architecture and architectural art as independent art forms comes from the writer Malraux in his book, *Voices of Silence*. He states that, "to the eyes of the artist, things are primarily what they may come to be within that privileged domain where they put on immortality but for that very reason, they lose some of their attributes: real depth in painting, real movement in sculpture." This process is

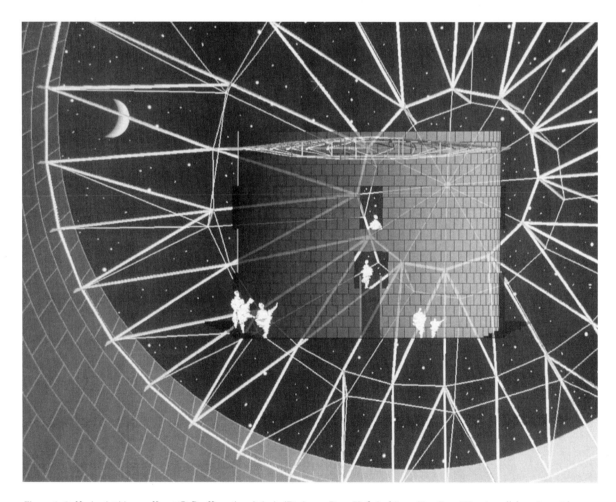

Figure 1–9. *Ho Am Art Museum, Kyung Gi-Do, Korea.* (1993) **Artist/Designer: Peter Huf. Architect: Kyu Sung Woo, in collaboration with Chris Haff.** Computer drawing.

The superimposed section provides the viewer with visual clues as to questions of form and scale without obscuring the representation of the roof structure—the real message of this arresting image.

26

identified by Malraux as *reduction* and called the very beginnings of art. He defined reduction as the process whereby an artist is forced to choose a self-imposed, self-limiting, set of parameters for creation. A painter is limited to two dimensions, the composer to the strictly aural, and the architectural designer to a lack of real abstraction. More importantly for Malraux, the artist's vision is formed early in life and conditioned by the objects or ideas of his or her passion; thus, the sculptor is primarily impressed by statues, the painter by paintings, the architect by buildings, etc. So then, the artist is in youth "more deeply moved by his visual experiences of works of art than by that of the things they represent—perhaps of nature as a whole."

In this, Malraux makes a deeply important point. To illustrate, if a landscape painter sits down to paint a sunset over the sea, a reasonably faithful representation of the scene may be produced, but the artist's efforts are ultimately informed more by *painting* than they are by nature. The red of the sky and the blue of the water may be the artist's inspiration for a representation, but the colors of the pigments are used as elements in a world—a separate, private, and viable world—that the artist builds with each brushstroke upon the canvas. While painting may be said to spring from nature, clearly painting is not nature; nor, for that matter, is nature to be equated with painting. The artist's voice exists, perhaps in tandem with but separate from the elements of inspiration. A painter of seascapes is not necessarily one who is primarily enamored with rocks and water, but one who at heart loves the *paintings* of these things above all. So, it is the architectural artist's paintings, not necessarily the buildings or even the ideas of the buildings, that may inform them and hold the key to the true significance of his or her work.

Drawing has often been compared to language, another form of idea communication. But, it is more to the point to assert that drawing *is* language just as are systems of words, numbers, or musical notations. Drawing is an attempt to establish a comprehensible order out of an otherwise jumbled barrage of perceptions and stimuli. Communication is the shared goal of any language, but in the various fields of the arts, something more is attempted—namely connection, explanation, interpretation, even enlightenment. The work of the poet Wallace Stevens was largely devoted to an examination, by means of the written word, of the concept of order. All human endeavor, perhaps consciousness itself, was for Stevens an attempt to cast a net of order over the essential chaos of life. In his "Anecdote of the Jar" he writes:

> *"I placed a jar in Tennessee*
> *and round it was, upon a hill*
>
> *the wilderness rose up to it*
> *and sprawled around, no longer wild."*

Figure 1–10. *Mnemotech Center. International Ideas Competition, Vittorito, Abruzi, Italy.* (1993) **Artist/Designer: Gordon Grice OAA, MRAIC. Architect: Mragna Architect, Inc.** Ink on mylar and pencil crayon on cronaflex, 66.6cm x 46.1cm

The simple, fluid drawn line as *language*—that of the written word as well as the visual image—is both the message and the artistic impetus of this compelling work.

The jar—the container—is a familiar and easily comprehensible thing and was used perhaps as a representation of a being, a consciousness, a life by Stevens as a locus, a randomly chosen station point from which to begin the process of comprehension and understanding of the world, any world, in which we might find ourselves. In Stevens' writing we can see elements of determinism and will at work but also the assertion of the Kantian idea that we primarily know the world by our relation to it. That is, we order our existence by means of what we know. "Life consists," Stevens writes elsewhere, "of propositions about life," and in this profoundly reductivist thought he captures both the idea of the positive stasis of the Absolute and the kinetic experience of art making.

"It is not enough to see architecture, you must experience it," writes S.E. Rasmussen, meaning that a photograph of a building is not a building and that we cannot know a building by merely studying images of it. This is because a lion's share of a building's nature is its very tangibility, its corporeal identity, and its use. Yet it must be remembered that seeing and experiencing an architectural painting is not the same as seeing and experiencing a building. Each act serves a different goal and has a different function. They are two separate but valid experiences which share elements of a common language, but are responsive to different, equally compelling voices.

No form of art-making can be said to necessarily enhance the process of artistic growth or evolution more effectively than another. To be truly successful, an artist must have an awareness of the interconnectedness, importance, and influence of artforms other than that which is his or her chosen means of expression. Still, it is as crucial to understand the differences between, as well as the similarities of, various forms of artistic endeavor. As Malraux points out, any form's "weakness" is simply a self-imposed limitation that is necessary to allow its strength to emerge. Perhaps to be most effective as a maker of art, or even as a conscious being, one has to be fortunate enough to suffer a bit from something like Fuller's early visual affliction. One needs to learn to see the world, and our place in it, in "big picture" pattern clues that allow us to glimpse through our endless manipulations of the specific, a promise of the infinite.

CHAPTER TWO

The Perfect Drawing

For those of us who have spent our lives attempting to complete the "perfect" drawing, one natural and understandable assumption is that we must, somewhere along the way, learn to draw perfectly. Armed with this somewhat naive and inductive conclusion in mind and a pencil or paintbrush in hand, a near-endless journey commences for the would-be artist.

Figure 2–1. *Untitled.* (1972) **Aldo Rossi.** Mixed media, 43cm x 40cm

Though at first glance, this work may appear deceptively "childlike" in its straightforward presentation of simple form, there is a more complex story hidden in the intentionally divisive composition and the conflict that is subsequently established with other representational elements. Notice the lone figure, silhouetted at the very center of it all.

Thinking that perfection must somehow lie in advanced knowledge and expertise, we see before us a daunting series of educational, technical, and intellectual obstacles to overcome the pursuit of "perfect" drawing skills, is an activity to which entire careers could be and are devoted. Of course, especially early on, we presume that if we travel this course successfully, we will be justly rewarded with the desired levels of expertise. But after some time we see that these hurdles, even if systematically and perfectly mastered, may not hold the key to the skills required to achieve the palest shadow of perfection. There is something missing and something which, even after years of study, one may still not possess.

Determining what constitutes the "perfect" drawing—of architecture or any other subject matter—ought to perhaps be the first avenue of study. But the answer to this mystery

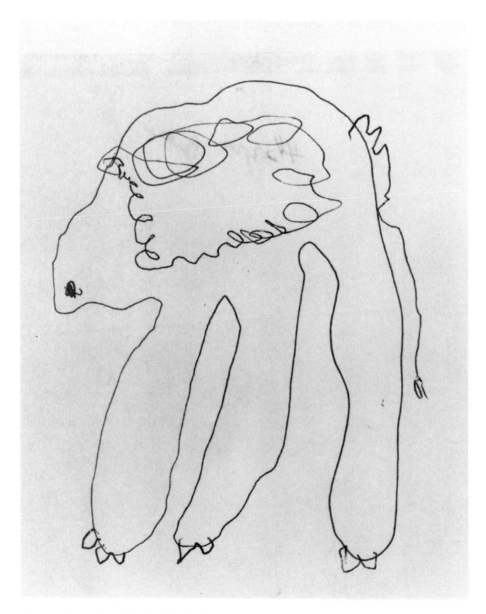

Figure 2–2. *Animal.* (1975) **Cathie Scholl.** Ink, 19.5cm x 19.5cm

The line perfectly describes objects by defining borders; what is in, what is out. In this case, the animal's lunch is allowed to emphasize the "inness" of the creature's contour.

In his indispensable book, *Art and Visual Perception: A Psychology of the Creative Eye,* Rudolf Arnheim examines the drawings of children in an attempt to discover the genesis of perception, the ways in which the human animal uses visual representation to express perception, and as a means of understanding perception itself. In his own study and investigation of the work of others—educators, psychologists, and art therapists—Arnheim convincingly argues that, far from being thoughtless exercises, the drawings of children are charged with meaning and clear representation. Moreover, he asserts that this representation is so clear as to appear abstract, even symbolic or conceptual. It is Arnheim's belief, however, that most children's work, despite our more adult preconceptions of "symbol" or "concept," is largely representational, albeit often highly stylized. He rejects the popular, so-called "intellectualist" or conceptualist theory, which delineates the division between perception and conception to explain why children draw the way they do. Simply put, this theory is

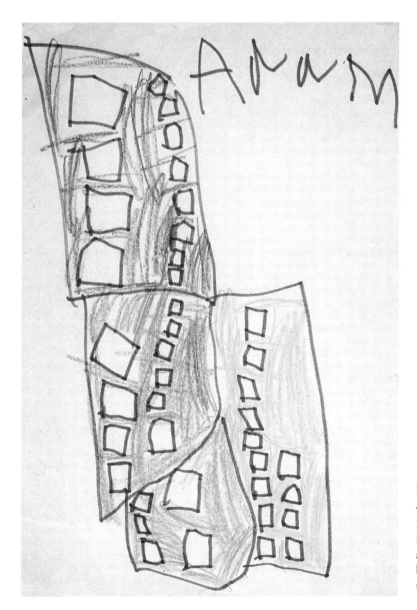

Figure 2–5. *Forty Story Building.* (1988)
Adam R. Decker. Marker, 30.7cm x 23cm

Despite any apparent abstraction, it is in fact conceptual representationalism at work here; the "fortyness" of the building acts as controlling inspirational factor.

based on the assumption that children draw what they see more or less exactly how they see it. Under this discipline, it is believed that children know the world and, therefore, represent it graphically, largely by relying upon non-perceptual, non-visual, and "abstract" concepts, such as language. So for instance, if a child were asked to draw a hand (relying on an example from Arnheim's book), the primary impetus would not be derived from the visual model of a hand but rather from the *idea* of a hand as represented by the knowledge of its having five fingers. The child would first and foremost grasp the "fiveness" of a hand and represent it graphically in an abstract way to caring little about the look of the drawing but taking great pains to be certain that the correct number of digits are present. Perhaps most adults would view the child's attempt as quaint and certainly as technically imperfect.

But by contrast, it is Arnheim's belief—the Perceptualist view—that while "fiveness" in this case may be crucial to the child, it is logically deduced purely by representational visual reference and not by any sort of language-based abstraction. Furthermore, it is for the child the real idea of "fiveness" that is paramount. It is not important, therefore, that the hand looks "perfect" but that it be perfectly represented. Figure 2–5 demonstrates material enough to fuel this debate. The drawing was executed by the author's young nephew following a conversation between the two on the topic of a forty story building. The artist, having rarely, if ever, seen a building of that size was very taken with the thought of such a monumental structure and determined to draw one. It is clear that the specifics of a particular building are less important here than is the representation of the generalities of a large building. Moreover, it is evident that, in this piece, "forty-ness" was the all-important reality for the artist to represent, as will be obvious to the reader who has the patience to count the exact number of windows shown. A conceptualist view would hold that the child's only input was the language-based conversation with his uncle; he constructed the entire image based upon purely non-visual input. By contrast, the perceptualist would argue that the child drew more upon his previous visually perceptive knowledge of both windows and buildings to complete his work. But clearly, it was the notion of "forty stories" that was most critical to him, which he went to great lengths to represent. Still, this is a representation of a building, not a symbol of a building. It is a generalized reality to be sure, but it is a real and not an abstracted concept.

Arnheim postulates that, despite appearances, children in fact do draw *what* they see, but more importantly, not necessarily *all* they see. They know something that endless study and academic pursuit can rarely teach the adult picture-maker—when to quit! Children know what to put in and what to leave out; in short, they know when a picture is *finished*. A drawing by a child may be simple not necessarily in betrayal of any lack of perception or insight or because of a simple absence of skill, but because according to Arnheim, "it fulfills all the conditions he expects the picture to meet."

Figure 2–6. *Resort Hotel, Portugal.* (1991) **T.W. Schaller. Architects: Arquitectonica.** Watercolor, 28cm x 43cm

A loose and high-spirited treatment with a bright watercolor palette was most fitting for the representation of this particular scheme.

In this light, how brave, beautiful, skillful, and communicative many so-called naive works begin to appear, and it is in their clarity and directness that many mature efforts at visual representation begin to pale. If we look again at the image previously discussed, perhaps we can begin to see something more than just a simplistic or charming image; the true essence of the subject matter emerges. If a more mature artist were asked to create a drawing based solely upon the phrase "forty-story building," how much "better" would the results be?

Later in his work, Arnheim asserts that perception begins with the *general* and proceeds to the *specific*. But perception does not, in his view, commence with specifics that are abstracted into generalities by the intellectual process. So then, it may be in the ability to

Figure 2–7. *"I–2 , Solo-Home."* (1995) **Artist/Designer: Willem van den Hoed.** Watercolor, 10.2cm x 15.3cm

This arresting image, in van den Hoed's words, depicts "an entirely closed building form. At ground level, the geometrical volumes that are subtracted from the box-shaped base form create an arcade. The wires define two semi-private spaces alongside the building [and] could also be read as communication links between the solo-home and the outside world."

Figure 2–8. *Castle.* (1993) **Benjamin M. Decker.** Marker, 25.6cm x 20.5cm

Fireworks and structure work together, in perfect balance, for an especially convincing overall atmospheric effect.

both grasp and represent the general, the *essential*, in almost any given subject that a child's drawing can astound even more than it can charm. And it is this ability, lost to most adults through the demands of the aging and educational processes, that can make their attempts at visual representation, while perhaps rich in technical skill and intricate detail, so wanting of spirit or ultimately even of substance.

In figure 2–8, we see what may be termed a simple representation of a castle. However, this artist (the younger brother of the author of the previous image, but having completed this work at a somewhat older age) has in fact truly captured the essence of the subject matter. Drawn shortly after a family vacation to a certain mid-Florida theme park, this image distills the central figure of the structure to its most elemental components. More interestingly, he composes the fireworks display as an element of at least equal importance to the architecture in the overall composition. The human figure, centralized but slipping off the page, is important, but is clearly secondary and, thereby, decidedly overwhelmed by the kinetic display. No ground line or plane is indicated, not because the artist lacked the skill or knowledge of the concept, but because it was not deemed sufficiently important to portray in the overall work. In fact, there is not one stroke in this piece that does not serve a purpose and which that should not be exactly where it is placed. Moreover, the lack of an apparent ground line gives the overall composition a more highly defined emphasis upon sky and atmosphere. Notice how the whites of the page, the negative spaces, have as much weight and importance as the rendered areas. This is a very effective technique that many older, more "skilled" artists would do well to study.

The expression of motion is another characteristic of many children's works, which is also addressed in Arnheim's work and clearly evidenced by the previous image. The fireworks quite literally explode off the page, their trailing light rays are almost diagrammatic of the idea of motion itself. Arnheim differentiates between expressive, physical, and descriptive, representational, movement in children's drawings. But these qualities can certainly be identified in more mature artists' work, of course, as well. It is Arnheim's view that children's need to be physically active carries through to their visual representations. He addresses the simple, primal joy of movement as it may be expressed in the creative artistic act. The purely physical motions that result in a representational "product" are, simply put, a lot of fun. Here too, this simple pleasure is all too often something that years of concentrated effort may dilute or steal away completely in the efforts of the adult. Happily though, this is of course not always the case as quite convincing examples of representational motion can be seen in the works of painters like Monet, Jackson Pollock, William DeKooning, and the more contemporary Eric Fischel, to name a few. The very brushstrokes in much of these artists' works vibrate, or leap off the canvas. In the world of architectural design, the concept sketches of London-based architect Zaha Hadid come to mind as especially representative of this idea. In the case of Hadid, though, her graphic representations are clearly an attempt to communicate, as tangibly as possible, her design sensibilities. That is, the sense of "movement" in her drawings would be only as important as is that same sense in the buildings she hopes to realize.

Interestingly, it is precisely because physical movement is so crucial to the child, that representations of movement in a child's work may be just as crucial. In figure 2–9 by yet another of the author's young nephews, the title, "The Wind," is apt enough. Arnheim and others would note the circular shapes as absolutely fundamental to the beginnings of visual perception, and, therefore, eventual representation—the primal circle—is the key concept. But it is here in the utterly appropriate and descriptive brush strokes that idea and perception come together in a near-perfect representation of mood and movement.

Figure 2–9. *The Wind.* (1993) **Thomas J. Sayers.** Watercolor, 30.5cm x 20cm
The sense, the feeling of a child's joy in movement, is perfectly captured here in a series of vigorous "primal" circles.

Figure 2–10 displays, for the author, a somewhat more troublesome problem in that it is one of his own earliest efforts. In an attempt to be as objective as possible, it must be said that an early facility and interest in depth of field, proportion, and perspective are evidenced here and that the journey from general to specific in representational terms had already begun in earnest. The subject was a nonexistent house (an early architectural utopian fantasy!) and its "ideal" inhabitants. While the general specifics of a house were undoubtedly provided previously to the artist by visual perception (unfortunately, not quite as successfully in the case of the sun, trees, or birds), it is the essential idea of a nonexistent "ideal" home represented here that may be of most interest: the connection between the drive it is toward, visual representation, and that of architectural design. The artist was intent upon representing a pleasing environment—trees, sunlight, birds, and a family enjoying all this, but most especially, their home—the essential focus of the picture (notice the relative scale of the figures). The artist, apparently pre-destined to a career in architecture and its representation, must have believed he was attempting to state that the "right" building could bring happiness—the American Dream of the post-war 1950s incarnate!

Figure 2–10. *House.* (1956) **T.W. Schaller.** Ink and crayon, 30cm x 23cm

It was not a specific house, but rather the idea of a "perfect" house that inspired this image.

An additional and final observation from Arnheim's work with children's drawings is the importance of the fact that the process of drawing or painting (and incidentally architecture itself) differs from photography in that it proceeds sequentially. It is, not unlike the very process of perceptual development itself, a cumulative art built up in stages whereby the result, but usually not the process, is seen all at once. This is especially critical for the artist to comprehend and remember since at heart it contains the simple truth that art is not so much in the paint as in the act of painting. In other words, the statement demonstrates that the *process* of art-making is as important, if not in fact more important, than the product of art-making. Therefore, if the process is true to the initial conception, then it must follow that the product will result in enhancing, rather than obscuring, the essential idea that fostered its inception.

Hugh Ferriss, the great American architect, artist, and visionary, urged architects and architectural artists to attempt to tell what he referred to as the "entire truth" about any building or environment which one might be called upon to draw. As previously stated, this "truth" for Ferriss consisted of both information and interpretation. Not surprisingly, tangi-

Figure 2–11. *"Ice"—Monsoon Restaurant and Bar Interior "MR 12," Sapporo, Japan.* (1990) **Artist/Designer: Zaha M. Hadid.** White crayon, ink, and acrylic on black cartridge paper, 20cm x 52cm

Less a drawing *of* a space than a drawing *about* a space, this image, like Hadid's actual structures, is the very embodiment of life and movement. Of the project she states, "The constraints of the conventional building [the existing structure enclosing Monsoon] created the desire to break away. The result is a hybrid of compressed, dynamic inside and static outside."

La finestra del poeta a MY. N.Y 78 AR
con la mano del santo

Figure 2–12. *La Finestra del Poeta a NY con la mano del Santo.* (1978) **Aldo Rossi.** Ink and marker on board, 30.5cm x 47cm

Though compellingly architectural, there is so much about this unique architect/artist's efforts in both built and unbuilt mediums that transcend any standard tectonic consideration. Architectural form acts as a mere springboard for other, far more subjective means of expression. The poet's window, for example, certainly opens to a much wider view of New York here than can be contained by any standard architectural language.

ble, objective architectural information is inherently more simple for most of us to portray graphically—for instance, the specifics of brick, stone, steel, or glass. Yet, since architecture is a sculptural, three-dimensional art form, it is insufficient for the artist to attempt to merely render physical facts upon the two-dimensional page. It is one art form attempting to fully express another. Therefore, Ferriss thought it essential that the architectural artist attempt to represent visually something of the feeling, the spirit, and the *essence* of the building being portrayed along with physical information in order to tell the full story— this entire truth. Just exactly how one attempts to go about this, the process of how to identify and hopefully to capture the elements of this essential idea, is precisely the aim of this book. For the contemporary artist, regardless of medium or subject matter, there are profound lessons to be learned from the works of Ferriss; through a gauntlet of sophisticated, often commercial architectural specificity and constraint shines the essential light of inspiration with a childlike clarity.

An understanding of the sequentiality of human creative endeavor was further illuminated by Arnheim via the writings of Baudelaire who writes, "A good painting, faithful and equal to the dream that gave birth to it, must be created like the world. Just as the Creation we see is the result of several creations, of which earlier ones were always made more complete by the next, so a painting, if handled harmoniously, consists of a series of superimposed pictures, where each new layer gives more reality to the dream and makes it rise another step toward perfection." Perhaps with a broader, more wholly inclusive approach to our work, those of us who spend our time attempting to produce better visual images may learn to develop, along with our continued efforts at technical expertise, a grasp of something of the "imperfection" of the child. What level and what types of information are needed in a developing work may become more evident to us, just as will those that are not. A grasp of the appropriateness and range of various graphic techniques may develop. The full story, which the work has to tell, may be allowed to emerge naturally, more clearly, and with less effort. In this way, what is truly *essential* in our work may become, to ourselves and our viewers, more perfect and more perfectly clear.

CHAPTER THREE

The Essential Idea: Objective Form

If, as we have seen, children may have the innate gift of expressing the "essential" in their drawings, is this ability necessarily lost with the passage of our years? In our inevitable journey from "the general to the specific" by means of age and learning, does this possibility simply wither and die or is it in fact "educated" out of us by the intensity we must give to the particulars of our chosen professions? Malraux states without equivocation that "the art of childhood dies with childhood and with the development of the will." Yet, while the actual ability to produce the art of the child must of necessity wane, it is more likely that the ability to see and, therefore to express, the "essential" is not so much lost to adults as it is obfuscated. We finally need to learn what we did not need to learn at first.

That this learning can and indeed should occur is clear enough upon a brief survey of the great art and artists throughout time. Almost without exception, what distinguishes a work of great art from a merely good or competent work, aside from and often even secondarily to a supreme command of technique, is the unassailable clarity of the artist's vision. Regardless of the complexity or technical mastery and sophistication of any work of art, it is the primary theme, the inspiration, the "essential," that shines through the entire composition and differentiates the great from good or merely competent work. It is this that above all should command the viewer's attention and respect. What exactly that one essential idea or vision may be varies, to be sure, from artist to artist, even from one piece of art to the next. For painters such as Rembrandt or Caravaggio, light as well as the symbolic meanings of light—truth, knowledge, apotheosis, redemption—defines the very essence of their work. It is this one supreme idea that reigns and, moreover, that is served by an astonishing range of technical command. This "primal light" is but one of the essential ideas that can be used by painters (to say nothing of the architects of the Cathedrals of the Gothic Period, for instance!). Color, tonality, form, composition, and tension are among the devices that can represent, symbolize, even act as the fundamental statement. For example, the concept of tension—the intentional dialogue established between two or more separate and contrasting ideas of equal importance—as is evident in the simple example of balance between dark and light, has been a highly favored device by painters throughout the history of art. The abstract expressionists of the 1950s were especially notable for their work in this area, but no less effective than these more modernist efforts are the elements of light/value which establish tension in paintings by Vermeer, Corot, and Mantegna.

Figure 3–1. *A West-End Club-House, perspective view with plans.* (1882) **Artist/Designer: Arthur Beresford Pite (1861–1934).** Pen and ink, 91.5cm x 63.5cm; Courtesy of The British Architectural Library, RIBA, London.

Shades of Beardsley and Durer as well as a heavy dose of Victorian-era Gothic resound through much of Pite's work, and while many of the day deemed this particular work loathsome, it did manage to secure for its author the RIBA's prestigious Soane Medallion in 1882. At the very least, this fantastic image succeeds in convincing the viewer of the communicative potential of an essentially line-based medium such as pen and ink.

Certainly no art form is excluded from discussions of the attempts to establish an essential theme—a single pure and overriding principle that defines the work and, it is hoped, shepherds the audience toward the desired goal of understanding, perception, and feeling. The disciplines of sculpture and poetry, no less than painting or architecture, are guided by this principle. Music utilizes many devices, not unlike those of painting—dynamic range, balance, tension, tempo, chromaticism—to represent and even to inspire a whole spectrum of intellectual and emotional response in the listener. The work of Beethoven is perhaps one of the clearest examples of the effective use of these properties in his large scale symphonic works. But think, too, of the clarity of vision and skillful shifting of key and color in smaller scale works such as the *Flos Campi Suite* of Ralph Vaughn Williams. Unlike many of the composer's other works, which have as their theme an almost otherworldly spirituality, this piece represents, almost replicates, the feeling of longing in the very secular search for earthly love. It is the artist's inspired choice to contrast a wordless human chorus with a distillation of earthy woodwind tones to create a study in sonority, which does not shy from the use of atonality to establish a palpably human mood and atmosphere. Choice here is the point—an

Figure 3–2. *The Renaissance in New York.* (1989) **Artist/Designer: Albert Lorenz.** Ink line, 93.6cm x 148.2cm
Few artists exploit the full potential of their chosen medium to the expressive degree of Lorenz. The fluidity, the contrast, and the sense of movement inherent in the simple, hand-drawn ink line are extrapolated within this highly thoughtful, witty, and sophisticated piece to inform the entire work. The artist succeeded in making the viewer believe that the drawing's playful, organic intent would have been impossible to capture as completely or appropriately in any other medium—a true *tour de force.*

Figure 3–3. *Assimilation.* (1993) **Artist/Designer: Gilbert Gorski AIA.** Etching, 20.5cmx 12.8cm

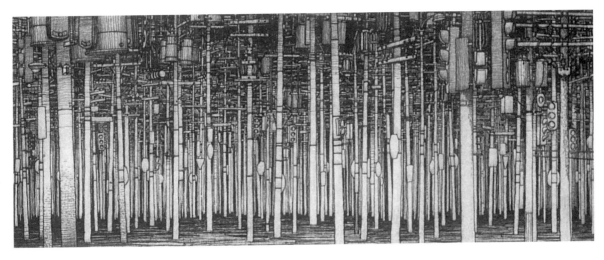

Figure 3–4. *Forest.* (1992) **Artist/Designer: Gilbert Gorski AIA.** Etching, 10.2cm x 25.6cm

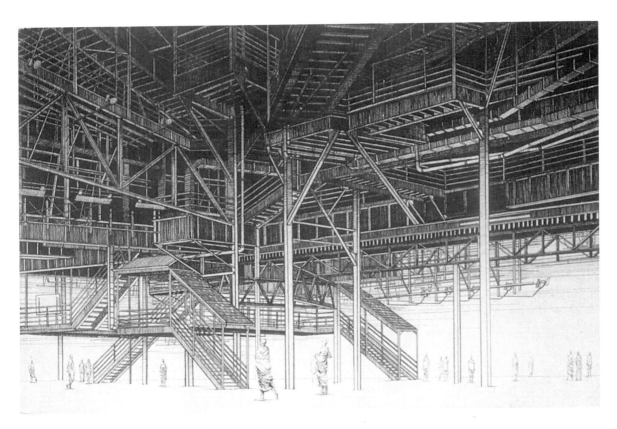

Figure 3–5. *Allometry.* (1993) **Artist/Designer: Gilbert Gorski AIA.** Etching, 17.3cm x 27cm

Gorski's sensibilities as both artist and architect consistently inform his work. These direct and remarkably expressive images are decidedly "architectural" in approach but, in addition, speak of a society's essentially chaotic search for order and "structure."

appropriate choice of means to achieve the desired end. These types of appropriate and successful choices can easily be experienced throughout the canon of recorded music, from the scoring and instrumentation of country and folk music to the sophisticated and subtle use of leitmotif in Wagnerian opera.

"Primal light" has recurred throughout the ages as a profound theme in architecture as well, but never more purposefully than in the Gothic Cathedral architecture of Medieval Europe. It is no exaggeration to suggest that the very stuff of light itself is as much an element in the design and construction of the cathedrals of Chartres and Salisbury, for example, as were stone or timber. As in more modern painting, the use of tension as a guiding principle recurs in examples of more contemporary architecture—perhaps as an appropriate response to or reflection of current social conditions. William Pedersen, in a recent essay appearing in *Kohn Pedersen Fox, Architecture & Urbanism 1986-1992*, defines an approach to the expressed duality of his recent design work as an intentional dialogue between harmony and conflict. Pedersen sees this duality or tension, which is one of his most central design themes, as largely inspired by the ancient Greeks' dualistic view of the world and the human condition. Represented to Pedersen by the symbols of the bow and the lyre is a balance between opposing extremes—black and white, good and evil, birth and death. Each instrument, one of war, one of peace, has an element under compression, the curved frame, and tension, the linear cord, and, thus, from each is issued its function and its beauty. Pedersen goes on to quote the great cellist Rostropovich as saying that composition consists of standard and exceptional parts and it is from the dialogue between the two that music can result. It is this same tension, this dialogue and juxtaposition of contrasting and similar elements, which so often gives a Pedersen building its singular grace, strength, and dynamic sense of purpose.

Figure 3–6. *J.F.K. International Airport Competition, New York, Interior Concourse View.* (1992) **T.W. Schaller. Architect: Kohn Pedersen Fox.** Watercolor and pencil, 42.9cm x 66.3cm

A commanding and primary interior vertical surface dictated the organizational structure of this graphic representation as well.

For the maker of architectural images, such discussions of the autonomy and interdependence of *content* and *intent* in a work could scarcely have more relevance. In the most real sense, when we say we are drawing a building, for example, it must be understood that we are in fact not drawing a building so much as we are drawing a *representation* of a building. As discussed previously, the intent and the content of an actual structure are, regardless of its subject matter, vastly different from that of a two-dimensional artwork. If we, as makers of images, set out to illustrate the qualities of a specific *building* rather than the qualities of a specific *drawing*, we will not succeed. A builder must use the elements of building to build, a painter, the elements of painting to paint. Architecture in its various guises has, more often than not, the building as its aim, whereas two-dimensional artwork, even when representing a building, has the image as its goal. So an artist, seeking to "paint a building," can never utilize the actual content of that building but must seek to represent the *intent* of the structure

Figure 3–7. *University of Pennsylvania.* (1992) **T.W. Schaller. Architect: Kohn Pedersen Fox.** Watercolor, 42.9cm x 66.3cm

A schematic stage aerial view of this developing design was completed to address generalities about context and volumetric concerns, and to avoid unnecessary and premature specifics.

by means of the *content* of painting—specific mediums, techniques, and approaches. It is precisely for this reason that many examples of architectural artwork are commonly thought of as inferior or secondary; at most, they are simply "art about art." The term "rendering" has an almost pejorative cast; the inference being that it is an attempt to "merely" depict, copy, or imitate. Yet even when at their most simplistically informational level, it is inaccurate to dismiss graphic visualizations of architecture as nothing more than derivative exercises. Architectural artwork is an attempt to freeze in time an image of something that, more often than not, does not yet exist. It is a unique discipline dealing with the intellectualization and visualization of a future material body. The artist must discern the *intent* of the proposed three-dimensional building by means of the *content* of the artwork, not that of the building, and communicate it clearly in two dimensions. Furthermore, that communicated intent must come to terms in some way with the intent of the artwork itself. It is here that the artist has the greatest challenge.

This intent, this governing principle must, as we have seen, be clearly identified and communicated in a work of art for it to achieve any measure of success, and no less so, in architectural artwork. The relationship a proposed building may be intended to have with its site, with the neighboring built environment, or between the elements of its mass and nega-

Figure 3–8. *International Terminal, O'Hare International Airport.* **Artist/Designer: Ralph Johnson FAIA. Architects: Perkins & Will.** Ink, 61.5cm x 92.3cm

tive space are all possibilities for the sense of intent which must be communicated in the visual image. The play of light, shade and shadow, reflectivity or absorption, color, and scale are other clues. The successful artwork has a lucid sense of prioritization—a clarity in its concept speaking to the viewer as to which elements must come of primary as well as secondary and tertiary importance. But while any good building may have a great many potent characteristics, a good image of that building must establish a hierarchy of representations of those characteristics, which will be most appropriate for that particular image, to tell its story effectively. All art of any kind is an attempt at storytelling. We tell the stories of our lives through our struggle to create art—who and where we are as well as who and where we wish to be. Artwork is a narrative that both represents and symbolizes the very process of living. Andre Malraux defines this process, "Artists do not stem from their childhood but from their conflicts with the achievements of their predecessors; not from their own formless world but from the struggle with the forms that others have imposed on life." The best narrative, like the best works of art—paintings, poems, symphonies, buildings—have a story to tell: one that most often proceeds logically from the beginning to the middle to the end, unveiling its purpose ultimately, at once, gradually, or at some point during the journey.

Figure 3–9. *International Terminal, O'Hare International Airport.* **Artist/Designer: Ralph Johnson FAIA. Architects: Perkins & Will.** Ink, 61.5cm x 92.3cm

Like Wright's unusually modernist images of the Larkin Building, for example, Johnson's characteristic graphics in stark, high contrast black ink line and tone emphasize the volumes created by offset and overhanging planar forms.

Perhaps the greatest challenge for any artist is to chose wisely from the available means by which to achieve the desired end. A medium must be capable of fully telling the story of the artwork without consuming it somewhere along the way. For instance, no one could deny the technical proficiency of Rembrandt, but if asked what one quality resonates after viewing an example of his work, the answer will usually be the light. Paints and canvas and brushes are the language of his story, but the light is the voice—the essential, the absolute, the destination toward which his work and his story proceeds. Similarly, it is the light that is remembered after a visit to the great Gothic cathedral at Chartres and not so much the tangible components of construction however impressive they may be. This was a building designed to be in service to a higher purpose. For example, following a performance of Beethoven's *Ninth*, Mahler's *Eighth*, or Wagner's *Parsifal*, one may be left with overwhelming exhilaration or sense of exaltation, but rarely a full recall of the specifics of tonal changes or orchestration. Here again, it is the story, the process, the journey, and the emotions it inspires that affect

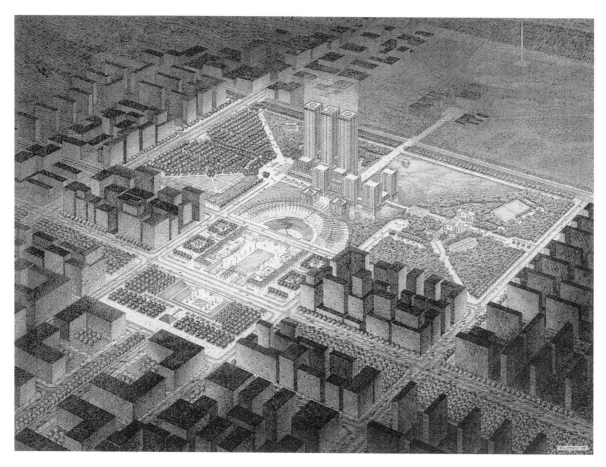

Figure 3–10. *Third Government Center Competition, Korea.* (1994) **Rael Slutsky AIA. Architects: Kunwon International, Seoul.** Pen and ink and color pencil, 76.9cm x 102.5cm

A dramatic and highly textured work, this piece was in fact largely created by a deceptively economical use of free-hand ink line; a technique which, in this case, silhouettes the subject area by means of light control. Notice the areas of the drawing that are *not* drawn are as important to the overall work as those that are.

one, not the technique by which that story is told. So, in any work of art, if the technique is allowed to dominate the essence of the work, the story it must tell risks becoming lost or subverted. Worse, a work can appear to be a story about its own technique—a form of "artistic cannibalism" to be stridently avoided. Of course, it will come as no real surprise that most

Figure 3–11. *Part Dieu Competition, Lyon, France.* (1992) **T.W. Schaller. Architects: Arquitectonica.** Watercolor and pencil, 70.2cm x 93.6cm

Similar but subtly differing towers are graphically treated in a near-elevational manner to heighten formal drama and allow the scheme to speak as lucidly as possible.

often, those artists with the highest degree of technical skill and mastery are the very individuals most capable of underplaying their technical gifts in service to the primary idea. That this ability may only be made evident through an advanced command of technical skills should be considered in light of the knowledge that this very ability is a synthesis of the skills of the intellect as much as of the hand.

The list of concepts of which the architectural artist or any maker of images should have an understanding, and at least some command, is long but can be reduced to a critical few for this discussion. Some of the most important of these are arranged below as a chronological journey from the most fundamental to the most complex. Works which incorporate elements from the latter end of the list must also embody those coming before it in a cumulative, evolutionary way, layering in a sense, one level over the next not incidentally, with transparency. This should not, however, imply that works which only utilize elements occuring earlier on the list are in any way necessarily inferior or less articulate. The photographs of Andreas Feinenger or the film, *The Third Man,* for example, could scarcely be accused of lacking refinement or insight because they avoid the use of color. A simple line drawing or an architect's rough conceptual design study not only may not benefit from considerations of tone or linear perspective, but may in fact lack impact or clarity as a result of

Figure 3–12. *Chicago in The Future.* (1993) **Artist/Designer: Manuel Avila.** Black ink and technical pen, 28.2cm x 43.5cm
The simple ink line is an expressive tool in the hand of this gifted artist.

58

their employment. Again, the message here is that one must choose the appropriate means to achieve the desired end. Greater levels, more layers, of sophisticated technique are often required to fully and correctly tell a visual story, but perhaps even more often that Miesian mantra, "less is more," continues to command respect and deserves to be followed.

The short list of concepts from which nearly all architectural artwork evolves is: space, line, light, color, and expression. It should be noted that these qualities share, for the sake of our discussion here, the rather simplistic framework goal of "object description." As a desired aim this in itself may rarely result in a superior work of art, but without knowledge of which an architectural artist may also be unable to achieve any loftier purpose. In later chapters, more specific works of art will be seen which incorporate all these qualities and more in various combinations to arrive at their stated goals. By design, this list is not intended as complete and is clearly subjective. Every artist is encouraged to discover those very personal elements of his or her own list of "essentials."

SPACE

An example of architecture, say a house, is most easily seen as an object existing in space. But upon any closer inspection we can easily see the holes in this seemingly fundamental fabric of perception. To begin with, our understanding of what a house is includes an awareness of the voids—the non-object spaces—within the volume of the object itself that gives it usefulness, function, and actual "houseness." So our supposed understanding of the structural-based "being" of the house must also include some knowledge of its void-based "non-being" as well. Speaking directly to this point, Rudoph Arnheim quotes the Tao Te Ching of Laotzu:

> "We put thirty spokes together and call it a wheel; but it is on the space where there is nothing that the usefulness of the wheel depends. We turn clay to make a vessel; but it is on the space where there is nothing that the usefulness of the vessel depends. We pierce doors and windows to make a house; and it is on the spaces where there is nothing that the usefulness of the house depends. Therefore, just as we take advantage of what is we should recognize the usefulness of what is not."

The words of Laotzu, proponent of "active negativism" or the "philosophy of intangibility," ring inexorably true and urge us as designers and architectural image-makers to take a closer look at what it is we do as well as at what we use to do it.

Amos Ih Tiao Chang interprets the philosophy of Laotzu for modern architects in *The Tao of Architecture*. To Chang, the true understanding of the concept of space is one of the primary elements left wanting by much of modern Western architecture. "The being of one thing," writes Chang, "is always made possible by the non-being of another thing. And real-

Figure 3–13. *Madison Square Garden Redevelopment Competition, New York.* (1987) **T.W. Schaller. Architects: Skidmore Owings & Merrill and Frank O. Geary.** Pencil, 70.2cm x 93.6cm

Very gestural and investigative, this sketch relied almost solely on a few rapid-fire lines of perspective construction to expeditiously convey the essentials of volume and form.

izing this, that the being of any form is created on the basis of non-being, and the architect acquires his maximum freedom of expression." In this statement Chang opens a door upon a breathtaking vista for all who are in any way involved in the act of art-making. The idea of the basis of art, of life itself, is hope—in a very real sense, a definition of space as an acceptance of the known as well as the unknown. The process of life depends upon a dualistic belief in the known and the not yet known as being interdependent, as one and the same thing. "Man is a living being," writes Chang, "He looks forward. He has hope. The complete reality in his mind includes, as well as existing objects, those intangible forms which will exist in the future . . . and because of the interaction between the objects man knows and those he does not know, the opportunity for developing the meaning of a new form is created. To him, the form of a new container expresses what it could be by expressing what it is not."

Figure 3–14. *Dakota Interior Perspective.* (1994) **Gregory T. Koester. Architects: Johnson/Wanzenberg.** Pencil, 46cm x 46cm
Simple, elegant line work conveys perfectly the essential design information of form and object in this sophisticated residential space. Exactly enough information is shown to effectively tell the story.

For the architect of course, but no less so for the artist who represents architecture, the need to understand space, the areas between, within, above, and below buildings as something other than a characterless "negative," or void, is critical. On the contrary, space can be viewed as a tangible entity charged with positive meaning, possibility, and even poetry.

Arnheim, too, stresses the distinction between two contrasting perceptions of space. One, *spontaneous perception*, suggests that "space is experienced as the given that precedes the objects in it, as the setting in which everything takes place." The second view, *relative perception*, stresses that "space perception occurs only in the presence of perceivable things" or that space is in fact actually created by existing objects. The first view, espoused by Plato, who defined space as "the mother and receptacle of all created and visible and in any way sensible things" and "the universal nature which receives all bodies . . . ," and Newton who described space as an "absolute base of reference against which all distances, velocities, or sizes have equally absolute measurements," is essentially a passive approach ascribing the definition of empty void nothingness to the concept of space. The second approach, far more in keeping with the thinking of modern physicists, tends to view space as having a far more active role in perceptual matters. It is, in fact, only because of the interstitial space within a grouping of buildings, for example, that we are able to fully discuss such relative concepts as height, scale, density, distance, and context. As image-makers it is only through an understanding of the potency of space that we can depict and even manipulate the visual representations of these concepts in our attempts to both compose a successful drawing and tell a building's story as fully as possible. Like Fuller, with his "pattern clues," we must attempt to appreciate both concept and context. Like the eponymous snowman in the poem by Wallace Stevens, we must attempt to behold the "Nothing that is not there and the nothing that is."

LINE

When the visual artist sets out to depict something on a blank piece of paper, an immediate, though not necessarily unpleasant confrontation must occur. In the discussions of relative space, we find that we can begin to know the nature of things as they compare to other things. The two-dimensional world of the drawing immediately determines, to some extent, the perceptual parameters of the representational world in which one can work, but it requires a belief or a suspension of disbelief on the part of the viewer. We must agree that what we see on a drawing table is not the "real" world but a "representation" of some aspect of it. We can choose to accept the world of the drawing as "real" and escape into it. Here, the paper represents space in a nearly Newtonian absolute sense and marks upon it as objects or interruptions within its expanse. By means of graphic devices, tonality, composition, and

Figure 3–15. *Telecommunications Tower, Jakarta* (1995) **T.W. Schaller. Architects: Skidmore Owings and Merrill.** Watercolor and pencil, 42.9cm x 66.3cm

The "negative" of space, sky, and environment in this image were modelled to define the initial "positive" form of the evolving scheme.

line, we can also choose to reflect our understanding and use the concept of relative, active space. But by far the simplest, most primal device by which the artist can begin to depict an object, or to differentiate between objects or areas of space, is the line.

Research into perception and child development tells us that the human mind, at least in attempt to communicate graphically, typically begins with the general and moves to the specific; the mind moves from the simple to the most complex. Hegel insists that only that which is simple constitutes a beginning, and in the process of visual representation, it is the act of drawing the single straight line that is seen as most elemental; the line is the genesis of graphic depiction whereby all visual artists' developmental process begins. Arnheim quotes Jean Cocteau, who makes the case convincingly when he states, "An artist does not skip steps, if he does it is a waste of time because he has to climb them later." So then, some understanding of the use and power of the line is fundamental for the graphic visualist.

Naturally, even before the line must come the coordinate—the point. Furthermore, since the straight line can most easily be understood as the shortest distance between two points, we come to grasp the idea of directionality. It is this perceived kinesthetic dynamic that begins to breathe life, a sense of representation, into even the simplest work. The empty page, the blank sheet of paper, begins to appear as a universe into which Cartesian coordinates are established against a Newtonian framework of "edges" to create locus points and their perceived visual connections, or lines, in an infinite variety of configurations—"constellations" to Arnheim. Limited by definition to the two-dimensions of the flat page, our eye can add an approximation of the third by means of the conventions of linear perspective and angularity, which will be discussed later. But it is by these methods and an artist's skill that, even in the limited world of the two-dimensional page, we can begin to see how space is not the Newtonian absolute, but rather is truly perceived and created by the shapes and objects involved with it. So, the concept of relative space again emerges.

Thus, the line can begin to be understood as more than a static mark on a sheet of paper; it can be perceived as an elemental function of the expression of space, or linear direction, with consequent implications of vector force, tension, compression, velocity, and mass. The line then begins to be seen as the fundamental building block of visual form, the boundary or edge which delineates one space, one form, from the next. In words that echo the teachings of Laotzu, Nietzsche observes, "The secret of form lies in the fact that it is a boundary; it is the thing itself and at the same time the cessation of the thing; the circumscribed territory in which the Being and the No-Longer Being of the thing are one in the same."

Clearly then, the line drawing lies at the very heart of visual representation. Using a deceptively simple binary system (on/off, plus/minus) of graphic depiction, the successful line work can suggest, in its economy, far more than it may show in fact. Breaking away from the straight line in his employment of sensual curves, Picasso constructed a world of meaning in his spectacular contour drawings. Again, the work of children when viewed in light of their apparent attempt to reduce visual and emotional stimuli to the most primal

Figure 3–16. *U.S. Federal Courthouse Competition, Foley Square, New York City, Rendered Elevational View.* (1993) **Elizabeth Ann Day. Architects: Kohn Pedersen Fox.** Watercolor, 102.5cm x 76.9cm

"Without the visual clues available to the artist in perspective drawings," writes Day, "it is essential to optimize, even exaggerate, the limited range of spatial cues in a rendered elevation to imply the three-dimensional form."

shapes and information in graphic form, can be appreciated on new levels. Of course, a good deal of architectural drawing imparts information on the basis of the most direct means available; therefore, there appears a pronounced reliance upon linework in conceptual sketch, more formal presentation, and technically specific orthogonal formats.

Little in the world of graphic communication could be seen as more dependent upon the use of the line than the orthogonal architectural drawing—plan, section, and elevation. These types of drawings are far more closely related to cartography—the straightforward communication of information in maps—than to pictorial or interpretative representation. As such, they are primarily stories about edges, directions, and boundaries. Examples of orthogonal work can achieve high levels of sophistication and craftsmanship, but it is usually their directness and austerity, their intended sense of removal and autonomy, that can give this type of work its beauty.

It is the very straightforwardness of the orthogonal drawing's communicativeness, usually without flourish, pictorial, or decorative intent, that establishes the truth of the assertion that drawing is the language of architecture. It is on this level that the relationship between the drawn image of a building and the written word can be established. An idea about design and an idea about spoken language are two methods of graphic communication that speak to the human mind by the graphic use of line. However, while there is interest in articulating the similarities between "drawn" and "written" means of communication, there is also danger in too emphatic an assertion of that sameness. While all means of communication rely on the use of symbols, the "written" learned symbols used to represent words or music, for that matter, differ significantly from those used to represent objects or space in that the latter also rely upon the viewer's universally presumed perception of the physical world. Moreover, and more importantly, while it may be possible, as Malraux points out, to conceive of a poet or philosopher or even a novelist who never physically writes a word, it is inconceivable to imagine a painter without paintings. Paintings or drawings are the visual artist's medium just as words are the poet's medium and music is the musician's medium. But because drawing or painting depends strictly upon sight rather than sound, its expression is, by definition, differentiated.

When one sees the written symbol for the word "circle," for instance, upon a page, the response is significantly different from the response recorded when one sees a drawn symbol for circle. The word "circle" can invoke many meanings, a circle of friends, a ring, and the idea of encircling. But the drawn image of a circle typically represents, at first glance, something a bit more general—a flat disc, a circular area, an object, a void, perhaps even a three-dimensional sphere. The difference lies in the fact that the drawing, no matter how simplistic, as opposed to the written word, which symbolizes an idea, is almost always a type of representation of the physical world. It is a thing. So, like the child who strives for the simplest, most economical means to represent the human form, more highly trained artists can see the Miesian "less" once again as being "more" in the primal circle. What is remarkable here, with regard to human visual perception, is the tendency to see the straight line not as static, but as directional, and the circle or square or any other shape not as simple lines or even connected vectors, but as edges, boundaries, which are most clearly descriptive of shape, space, and object.

When the artist first commits pencil to paper, it is important to remember that, as Arnheim points out, there is, in point of fact, "no such thing as the strictly flat, two dimensional image." Conventions of visual perception deeply inform the ways in which we react to a drawing—no matter how simplistic. Even if that work is composed of just a few abstract-

Figure 3–17. *Singapore Performing Arts Center Competition, lobby view.* (1992) **T.W. Schaller. Architects: Kohn Pedersen Fox.** Watercolor and pencil, 28cm x 43cm

A gestural treatment of architectural form emphasizes the great expanse of light-filled interior space—the focus of this design.

Figure 3–18. *American Museum of Natural History, Hayden Planetarium, entry vies, New York.* (1995) **T.W. Schaller. Architects: J.S. Polshek and Partners.** Watercolor, 28cm x 43cm

This vignette was one of a larger series of "intimate," hand-done drawings which were deemed the most effective way to explore the approach and entry sequence experience of this site-sensitive proposal.

looking lines, they are not simply lines on a surface, but rather lines in three-dimensional space. This is great news for the architect and especially for the architectural artist in his or her attempt to portray buildings in space. It was not so helpful, however, to abstract painters such as Mondrian who experimented with spatial hierarchy and visual perception in an attempt to create a perfectly "flat" image. Even in his most detached works, one line or band can always be seen as passing over or in front of another, creating the recurring image of object and empty space.

In the world of architectural representation, the tenets of visual perception come most clearly into play within the realm of linear perspective. The ways in which we perceive objects and space in the real world are represented—sometimes even symbolized—by the ways in which we draw them on the page. These perceptual tenets are never more succinctly represented than by means of the line drawing. Cartesian geometry teaches that the three major coordinates—width, depth, and height (x,y,z)—are all of equal importance. However, upon the face of Earth, such is not strictly the case. Gravity dictates that the vertical rules; furthermore, that mass arranges itself about the vertical axis in a building. Thus, horizontality and verticality in architecture can easily be seen as assuming symbolic meaning; for instance,

Figure 3–19. *Megaworld Place, Manila.* (1996) **T.W. Schaller. Archtiects: Skidmore Owings and Merrill.** Pencil, 43cm x 33.15cm

This preliminary pencil sketch was quickly completed as an overlay of a CADD image to readily communicate the primarily design intent prior to a more "finished" presentation.

Figure 3–20. *Fixing Our Future.* (1996) **Artist/Designer: Gordon Grice OAA, MRAIC.** Ink on mylar, 46.8cm x 46.8cm; Courtesy of Rod Morris, Morris Marketing; commissioned as cover piece for Toronto Business Annual.

This exuberant work takes a decidedly editorial approach to the use of architectural imagery as directly expressed in pen and ink, animating those typically static forms to convey information—and opinion—with skill, humor, and utmost clarity.

the ideas of stability and risk of holding or reaching upward. Therefore, as we view and come to spatially understand our world, we assign a hierarchy to directionality—the vertical being first, the horizontal second, and the diagonal a distant third. So, as we represent our world in drawing, our mind instinctively arranges the system of lines for us, telling us which ones are perpendicular to the earth, which ones reach out along the ground plane or are parallel to it, and which ones are tangent or angular. Since the vast majority of building artifices depend upon the right angle, the vertical, and the horizontal, and since our spatial perception also relies primarily upon those two concepts, then, in drawing, the angled line is the one which most often recedes into space; it is the representation of perspective.

Of course, in nature, neither the truly straight line nor the parallel vertical line can, in fact, exist. In the world of visual representation, the lines are conventions or inventions of the human mind and thus establish order upon the chaotic wealth of received visual stimuli. All methods of drawing, architectural or otherwise, represent accepted forms and conventions of representation. Most people, with or without architectural training, can understand the plan, section, or elevation of a house, for instance, without having to be told that one can never, in fact, see a house in precisely any of these ways. Still, more people can understand a simple linear perspective sketch of the house without skill or technical knowledge of perspective construction. These drawings are effective tools for establishing concrete design communication; moreover, they are fascinating examples of how, as human beings, we organize our perceptions of the world around us in simple but exceptionally rich visual terms.

CHAPTER FOUR

The Essential Idea: Subjective Expression

The exploration of the essential constituents in image-making is expanded in this chapter with an investigation of some less tangible elements of visual representation—light, color, and finally, expression. Again, these are not qualitative designations meant to suggest that they are necessarily better ways to describe objects than are the fundamental concepts of space or line. Still, they cannot simply be characterized as other methods of graphic depiction. After all, they do depend upon, or are in a sense evolved from, the elements of our earlier discussion. So, in this regard, they are in some way a more sophisticated manner to attempt the representation of architecture; but, as always, appropriateness is the key. While the skills to understand and manipulate the qualities in the completion of artwork should be at the artist's disposal, each skill or all of them are not always the best choice for any given condition or work of art at hand.

Figure 4–1. *The Tomb of Merlin.* (1814) **Artist/Designer: Joseph Michael Gandy.** Watercolor, 76cm x 132cm; Courtesy of the Trustees of Sir John Soane's Museum and The British Architectural Library, RIBA, London.

Light was the "essential" idea, the emotional touchstone, of much of this great Romantic artist's output and never more evident than in this astonishing work of art inspired by Ariosto's *Orlando Furioso.* The cold, dark stone of the tomb is transformed here into a great source of light, warmth, and life which is visually and symbolically rich in meaning.

LIGHT

Whereas the line drawing attempts to explain the shapes or extent of an object or a space by describing boundaries or *edges*, the tone drawing accomplishes this task by an emphasis on delineating *surface*. The primary difference between these two approaches is in the latter's consideration of the properties and effects of light. While it may certainly attain a high level of representational sophistication, line-based work must always, by definition, be seen as a some-

Figure 4–2. *BMC Real Properties Building, Houston, Texas.* (1993) **Douglas E. Jamieson. Architects: Keating Mann Jernigan Rottet, Los Angeles.** Airbrush, 102.5cm x 76.9cm

Despite this artist's great facility with color, the subtle tonal variations of the design scheme suggested this deft treatment in black and white. Note the inclusion of the orthogonal elevation used as backdrop for the perspective—a brilliant mix of the rational and the romantic.

Figure 4–3. *Nagoya Building, Nagoya, Japan.* (1992) **T.W. Schaller. Architects: Kohn Pedersen Fox.** Pencil and pastel, 43cm x 28cm

Silhouetting the subject building as a light focal point against a dark surround serves the dual purpose of establishing clear visual identity and of allowing design specificity to be avoided in a developing scheme.

what abstract aproach insofar as we do not visually perceive the world as a simple system of edge or boundary lines. Of course, it is important to restate that this abstraction can be the great strength of line work rather than a shortcoming. There are times when this sense of distillation and remove are entirely appropriate and desirable by telling its stories so directly. Architectural floor plans, for example, or highly schematic perspective sketches are most communicative in line form; they are perhaps closest to our intellectual understanding of object and non-object, being and non-being. However, when the attempt is to approximate more closely in graphic terms, human visual perception, considerations of light, and tonality must come into play. Only in this way are we able to more fully explore those grey areas between absolute being and non-being undulations of light that constitute our physical world.

Without considerations of light, discussions of visual perception become moot; for indeed, without light, we can visually know neither object nor space. Light is among the most primal of all human experiences, and as such, any considerations of it come with implications of near mythic proportion. As subject matter, light has inspired endless artistic and intellectual debate in an attempt to grasp its physical, emotional, and spiritual nature. That architects throughout the ages have attempted to capture and subsequently utilize the effects of light in their efforts to create more pleasing or effective building types, does not come any surprise. For both utilitarian and more purely decorative or expressive purposes, builders have long recognized the power of light, or more directly, the power of the Sun. It was the mythic power of the sun that was harnessed, for example, to illuminate the great interior of the Pantheon in Rome. The light was directed to instruct and to express the power and meaning in the planes of the sculpture and in the coffers of the great dome ceiling. The light was controlled and subdued by the deep, heavily columned portico, and made the luminescence of the interior just that much more astonishing.

Corbusier liked to quip that he "designed with light;" never was this more profoundly true than as seen in his Chapel at Ronchamp, a masterful example of "light composition." Within the relatively dark interior, the size, location, and configuration of the openings in the massive walls act to identify the space, to be sure. However, it is the highly controlled and directed light, which penetrates these openings, modulated by the thickness and color of the glass, that because of the architect's skill, quite literally creates the art of this great architecture. One is reminded of that other gifted orchestrator of light, Louis Kahn, who wrote, "We only know the world, the world as it is evoked by light, and from this comes the thought that material is spent light." Again Kahn, speaking even more directly to the point, writes, "The sun does not realize how wonderful it is until after a room is made. A man's creation, the making of a room, is nothing short of a miracle. Just think, that a man can claim a slice of the sun."

Painters too, in representative form, can be said to "paint with light." Turner and Rembrandt seemed, for example, to more explicitly paint light itself in their dramatic chiaroscuros, fully exploiting the literal and metaphoric meanings of *light* and *dark*. A com-

(left) **Figure 4–4.** *J.F.K. International Airport Competition, New York, Baggage Level View.* (1992) **T.W. Schaller. Architects: Kohn Pedersen Fox.** Watercolor and pencil, 42.9cm x 66.3cm

The attempt to allow natural light to penetrate the lower level in this proposal was also to become the essential idea of this resultant image.

(below) **Figure 4–5.** *J.F.K. International Airport Competition, New York, Aerial Perspective View.* (1992) **T.W. Schaller. Architects: Kohn Pedersen Fox.** Watercolor and pencil, 78cm x 117cm

This image's composition and dramatic modeling of value range is an effort to underscore the signature design inspiration—the shape of a wing.

parison of the work of these two painters reveals the infinite potential of both an artist's work, with representations of the dramatic effects, as well as the expressive potential of light itself. While the light in a Turner is an explosive, indomitable force, a breakthrough, an insight, and a force larger and more powerful than the darker elements of Nature; in contrast, the light in a Rembrandt reveals itself gradually, bit by bit, as if struggling soberly but nobly against the inevitability of the darkness, and this light knows it will vanquish all in time. Upon reflection, it is clear that the *light* and the light these two men painted had less to do with any actual physical properties than with the emotional or spiritual struggles expressed by light, which each artist felt was best represented by conflict, the juxtaposition of darkness and light.

This Manichean dualism can be as much evidence in an example of fine architectural artwork as it may be in any superb building or exceptional painting, where the precise forces of light and dark are at work. One cannot help but to be reminded of the light-infused efforts of Piranesi or Ferriss. Tonalities, which help explain the physical characteristics of the envisioned structure as well as the intentions, interpretations, or sensibilities of the architect/artist, can gain an expressive forum not readily available to or evident in the line-based work. It is precisely here, in this emotionally expressive forum, that architectural artwork takes its most substantive and, to be fair, controversial step forward. The non-tone based line drawing, even the linear perspective, used to depict architecture, must, by definition, always aspire to the physical and the technically descriptive aspects of design. As stated, such drawings are by no means inferior or necessarily less sophisticated than ones which utilize tone; on the contrary, they are often more appropriate to the task at hand. However, when tonalities are introduced in a work, an expressive line has been crossed. Appropriateness of usage is a consideration that cannot be over stressed. Typically, a toned orthogonal drawing of construction details would be specious, even confusing, to a contractor attempting to erect a building. Yet, remember that students of the École des Beaux Arts routinely pochéd the wall thicknesses and sectional cuts on competition drawings almost entirely in the name of descriptive clarity. The obvious distinction lays in the fact that drawings completed for display have a different purpose, a different audience, than drawings executed for construction. A plan drawing of a house, for example, could be delineated in various methods depending upon the viewers it is intended to reach—a straightforward and fully dimensional line drawing for one interested group, or fully rendered and complete drawing with cast shades, shadows, and suggested furniture placement for another. Similarly, a perspective view of the same house, articulated with the play of light and dark might mean very little to one who is building, or even designing, the structure, but a great deal to one who may eventually come to live in it.

The dualistic nature of architectural artwork, the often complimentary and sometimes conflicting need to explain as well as to express, is seen clearly in the perspective-based tone drawing. Is this type of work the artist's attempt to allow the viewer to understand the specifics of the structure itself or, rather, is it an attempt to convey a sense of what one might

Figure 4–6. *I.M.C. Office Tower, Kuala Lumpur.* (1992) **T.W. Schaller. Architects: Tsao & McKown.** Watercolor, 70.2cm x 93.6cm

A full night view was chosen here as an "evasive tactic" or an appropriate graphic response to a design scheme whose sculptural form was nearly set but whose surface materiality was far from being decided upon.

Figure 4–7. *First Citizen's Bank and Trust Company Headquarters, Raleigh, North Carolina.* (1990) **T.W. Schaller. Architects: Kohn Pedersen Fox.** Pencil, 78cm x 117cm

An informal and investigative sun angle and value sketch of this formal proposal inadvertently creates a compelling study in contrast.

feel in the presence of the specific building once completed? Clearly, it can be both. In so doing, the very nature of architectural design has been defined—the collaboration between the tangible ideas, realities, and the abstract. In the architectural structure, wrote Nietzsche, "man's pride, man's triumph over gravitation, man's will to power, assume a visible form. Architecture is a sort of oratory of power by means of form."

The architectural drawing can document, interpret, even forecast this journey of architectural identity and expression in its unique ability to tell Ferriss' "entire truth" about structure—its tangible, physical presence as well as its intangible spiritual self or its soul. The use of tonality is the oratorical threshold which bridges between the necessary realm of explanation and the less clear but no less crucial realm of expressive possibility.

COLOR

Differences of tonality within an existing structure have a fundamentally different nature than the shifting tonalities within a painting or drawing of a structure. Ignoring, for the moment, tonal differences between any given building's selected construction materials, shapes and volumes in a building are differentiated to the human eye by the play of light upon surfaces. The tonalities in the two-dimensional work of art are *representations* of that

Figure 4–8. *Strivers Center, Harlem. New York City.* (1992) **T.W. Schaller. Client: NYC Economic Development Corporation.** Watercolor, 70.2cm x 96.3cm

One of a series of "non–architectural" and atmospheric images—this view was completed in an attempt to gain community, political, and developmental interest in the potential renaissance of this inner city neighborhood.

play of light, just as the shapes of the structure itself in a drawing are *representations* of those shapes. Indeed, it is the effective representative delineation of the effects of light that allows the shapes to be seen at all in the successful tone drawing. It is valid, then, to discuss the addition of color in architectural artwork as being not an alternative method of delineating shapes or objects, but rather as another perhaps more complete or evolved method. For while the tone drawing may not utilize color, out of necessity the color drawing must almost always use tonality.

This statement is consistent with thinking that accepts the premise that perception proceeds from the general to the specific, from the simple to the more complex. This logic sug-

Figure 4–9. *II–10.* (1995) **Artist/Designer: Willem van den Hoed.** Watercolor, 10.2cm x 15.3cm

The prolific Dutch-based architect/artist, Willem van den Hoed, incessantly explores architectural form and function in log books in which he quickly jots down thoughts and impressions—much like in a design-based visual diary. This piece is one of a series of possible combinations of a linear base form combined with other shapes.

gests that the tone of an object, in human visual perception, is more important that its color. In fact, however, visual perception is less concerned with color or specific tone than it is with shape. That being said, tone is, nonetheless, simply a better, more primary indicator of shape than is pure unmodulated color. When concerned with ordering our visual environment, ". . . shape," writes Arnheim, "is a better means of identification than color; not only because it offers many more kinds of qualitative difference, but also because the distinctive characteristics of shape are much more resistant to environmental variations."

Without doubt, most of us can identify shapes, say that of a house or the human figure, from a near-infinite variety of angles or under a variety of lighting conditions, regardless of considerations of color. But for the artist, the act of recognizing or identifying objects is generally no more important, sometimes even less so, than is the intellectual or emotional response which may be caused in the viewer. For this response, shape, tone, and mostly color, are all essential; each of these qualities has unique but interrelated characteristics. For example, if shape identification is little affected by the properties of illumination, then tone and color are, by contrast, deeply dependent upon these properties. To be more precise, in a

Figure 4–10. *Interior of an Egyptian Temple.* (1928) **William Walcot (1874–1943).** Pencil and gouache, 80cm x 104cm; Courtesy of The British Architectural Library, RIBA, London.

This piece is representative of Walcot's vigorous and eclectic approach to both his graphic endeavors and design interests as well. Bold, impressionistic mixed media "events" describe many of his images which, like this one, combined architectural fact and fiction to near-visionary result.

painting color is *affected* by illumination whereas tone *is* illumination. An object may be *identified* by shape but it may not be able to be fully *understood* in a painting, if not for tone and color.

Articulating the traditionalist view that shape precedes color in perceptual importance was Matisse, who wrote: "If drawing is of the spirit and color of the senses, you must draw first, to cultivate spirit and to be able to lead color into spiritual paths." This statement, by no less than one of the finest of all colorists who ever lifted a paintbrush, defends the classicist view of shape and form as dominant over color. Arnheim compares the work of the painter Delacroix, who approached painting in more "romantic" terms by emphasizing the expressive qualities of color and shape with that of Jacques Louis David. Ever the classicist, David created in solid, noble, and static shapes, which were further clarified by subdued use of color. Kant, too, as deduced from Arnheim's notes, had much to say about shape as "the foundation of taste," while he believed that colors "belong to the stimulation" of the senses. He went on to discuss color as "entertainment" and to say that color may "animate the sensation of the object but cannot make it worthy of contemplation and beautiful."

Qualitative and judgmental discussions of the use of color in art notwithstanding, it can hardly be argued that color usage is without merit or superfluous to the maker of images. On the contrary, it is often essential. For the maker of architectural images, beyond attempts at simple material description, color can be a powerful tool for effective storytelling.

That the viewer of a work of art may have an emotional response to the artist's use of color does not come as a surprise. But for the architectural artist attempting to fully represent the idea of design, this is a fact as worthy of study as is the intellectual response a viewer may have to graphic representations of shape and form. Colors do far more than describe, they affect. A painting dominant in the hues of the red range will be received much differently than one executed primarily in the blue range, even though the objects and shapes described in both may be the same. The "red" work can be said to be warmer while the "blue" work is termed "cooler." These so called "temperature" differences have nothing to do with any innate quality of the specific color, but everything to do with the emotional response they produce in the viewer. It should be pointed out that pure saturated colors, such as red or blue, for instance, have, as Rudolf Arnheim states in *Art and Visual Perception,* little temperature identity. The admixtures of color that establish these distinctions; a reddish blue, for example, may seem a "warmer" color than a bluish red. It is only then that the dynamics of a color, its direction perhaps, dictate its temperate identity and, thereby, its ability in artwork to cause an emotional response.

Anthropologists have discerned that most primitive languages distinguish only between darkness and light, and all colors are assigned to one or the other of these two polar designations. When a language develops a name for a third color, it invariably represents the color we call red. It is then not incorrect to think of red as a primal color, representing, as it often

View at Street Level

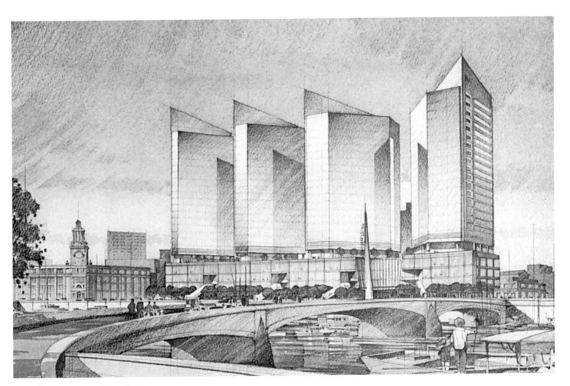

View from Opposite River Bank

Figure 4–11. *Waytufund Competition, Shanghai, China.* (1996) **T.W. Schaller. Architects: Fox & Fowle.** Watercolor and pencil, each: 42.9cm x 66.3cm

A vital and active waterfront atmosphere was the impetus for this proposed design as well as the essential idea behind the compositional and media use choice for the images.

does, passion, the secular, and the most instinctive and elemental of impulses. Volumes have been written on color perception and theory, and it is not prudent or, for that matter, possible to attempt here a summation of all scholarship on the subject. But perhaps it best serves the scope of this book to turn to a study of the work of an individual who, ironically, does not, in the usual sense, paint or draw.

Figure 4–12. *American Museum of Natural History, Hayden Planetarium, Night view from park, New York,* (1995) **T.W. Schaller. Architect: J. S. Polshek and Partners.** Watercolor, 28cm x 43cm

The striking concept of a glowing orb in a transparent box was attempted here in the most direct and expositional manner.

Cinematographer Vittorio Storaro has a deep belief in and commitment to the use of color in his work. Probably best known for his Academy Award-winning efforts on the Francis Ford Coppola film, *Apocalypse Now,* and Warren Beatty's film *Reds,* he is perhaps most eloquent in the collaborative work done with his fellow Italian director, Bernardo Bertolucci. Such cinematographic gems as *The Last Emperor, The Sheltering Sky,* and *Little Buddha,* would be far less notable without his condiderable talents. Far more than a photographer of preexisting elements, Storaro sets scenes and compositions with, quite often, color as the dominant rather than the supporting or decorative theme. Color is allowed, even encouraged, to establish its own narrative, sometimes in support and sometimes in addition to the primary narrative of the script. Storaro sees color as profoundly vocal and informative and he speaks of life itself as essentially a "spectral journey."

We begin in darkness and end in light, Storaro says; thus, pre- birth and death are colorless, immobile states of being or rather non-being. Life for him, in fact *is* color; and hence, the journey of life, symbolized by movement along the spectrum of color, is art. The colorless black unconsciousness of non-being is pierced by the first light of life—red, the most primal of colors—symbolizing for him life's first awakening and most primitive urges. For Storaro, orange and yellow appear next and represent the beginnings of awareness, consciousness, and family. Green is central to Storaro's work, and not surprisingly, falls squarely in the center of the color spectrum. He indeed sees it as the middle, as the center of awareness, and as youth interacting with age—a growing awareness of later knowledge. For him, blue is the color of intelligence. Much of Storaro's work is concerned with the tension, the dialogue established by the "passion of red" conflicting with the "reason of blue." Indigo and violet come next along the spectrum and are representative, for Storaro, of insight, wisdom, and acceptance that may come with old age. Finally, he sees death as the color white, the pure light, the end of the journey, the enlightenment of the meeting of all color, and the final stasis of Joyce and Aquinas.

Figure 4–13. *TCU Performance Center, Theater, Fort Worth, Texas.* (1994) **T.W. Schaller. Architects: Hardy Holzman Pfeiffer.** Watercolor and pencil, 43cm x 66.3cm

This is one of a series of design development drawings done to explore the visual atmosphere created by this and several other of the unusual performance spaces planned for the facility.

As an example of application, in the film *The Sheltering Sky*, entire sections of the work were shot with a dominant red or blue cast created by lighting and filters. This was done not only to affect the viewer but to represent in a narrative sense a particular character's state of mind at the time. The first character, "red," was following the sun, it was hoped, toward enlightenment. Unfortunately, it was reached, in his case, in the form of death. The second character, "blue," followed the moon toward knowledge or understanding. Sadly, she reached only madness. In the field of music composition, echoes can surely be heard in Storaro's approach to the use of musical *leitmotif*—character specific themes or tonalities which establish identity conflict or resolution.

Just as life is a spectral journey for Storaro, the pure, primal colors black and red-orange in art represent the past, while blue symbolizes the violets, and white symbolizes the future, the destination, and the Absolute. While the reader is, of course, encouraged to study this man's films, it is not so much to witness the literal ways we may utilize color in our own artwork, but to discover some of the potent responsibility any color or combination of colors may have in affecting the viewer. In short, color can do far more than simply decorate or describe, and a range of color can establish a world of dialogue and meaning. When we attempt to represent an image of architecture in color, we should deeply consider the entire palette of the overall work of art as much as the color of any specific object that may be the focus of the piece.

INTERPRETATION *and* EXPRESSION

In the preceding pages, we have looked at a very few of the techniques or possibilities open to the artist in search of the "essential" in a work of art. Of course, there is a myriad of other possibilities. Kinetics or movement, various moods or emotional states of mind such as light-heartedness, sobriety, formality, or a sense of mystery, rock-like solidity, or sail-like lightness, even metaphor or symbolism, are all examples of some of the guiding principles that can help structure, guide, or inform a work.

If we do come to see drawing as storytelling, then a great many useful drawing lessons can be discerned from the study of literature and other "narrative" arts such as music, as mentioned earlier. Wagner conditioned his listeners to recognize specific qualities about particular characters through the use of *leitmotif*, assigning certain musical themes or chromatics to only one character or group. True, this is openly manipulative and the composer has been roundly, and often rightly, criticized for the choices he often made with the types of ideas or characters he "painted" in a charitable or unfavorable musical light—for example, *Die Meistersinger von Nuremberg*. Still, such explicitly thematic and narratively composed music, though common today, was amazingly progressive in the mid-19th century and is, in any

Figure 4–14. *First Metrobank, Manila, lobby view.* (1996) **T.W. Schaller. Architects: Kohn Pedersen Fox.** Watercolor and pencil, 42.9cm x 66.3cm

A sense of strong natural light was allowed to mold and dissolve the representation of the clear architectural forms, which were themselves a subtle contrast of warm and cool tonalities.

Figure 4–15. *The Large Glass: Hancocked Tower.* (1990) **Tamotsu Yamamoto.** Graphite pencil, 76.9cm x 102.5cm; Courtesy of Mr. & Mrs. Paul J. Carroll AIA.

Of his subtly alarming image, Boston-based architect/artist Yamamoto states, "Marcel Duchamp added a moustache and goatee to a reproduction of the most famous painting in the world, Mona Lisa, and years later he signed an unaltered print of it, subtitling it, *Rasee*—French for "shaved."

case, a perfect example of the "essential" in art-making. At its best, it is undeniably deeply effective, non-verbal storytelling.

Beautifully nuanced writing, such as is found in the books of Kazuo Ishiguro, again establishes the effectiveness of thematics and a clear identification of central "essential" ideas in art-making. In his novels, such as *Remains of the Day, Artist of the Floating World,* and *The Unconsoled,* Ishiguro is most skillfully doing more than simply relating a compelling story. He is establishing a mood, a tone, which is appropriate in each case to the characters and events of his work.

Often, the word or phrase implied but left unsaid can tell far more about a character's sense of alienation and remoteness than pages of descriptive text. With a deft and economical choice of words, Ishiguro sets a tonal *leitmotif* as effectively as Storaro or Wagner without a character ever having to utter a word.

What we come to see is that every word of an Ishiguro novel, every brush stroke of a painting by Rembrandt, and every note of a Beethoven symphony is included for a purpose. Nothing is extraneous, and moreover, every move and every small element of these works of art exists to create the whole, which, because of craft and inspiration, often exceeds in impact the sum of its various, however well-designed, components. These "art-stories" succeed because of the clarity of the artist's vision and the effective directionality of elements. So, it is not sufficient for the artist to identify an "essential," a "main theme," in a proposed work. It remains that the various lesser themes or components must be identified, orchestrated, and

Figure 4–16. *The New York Botanical Garden, Children's Adventure Garden, New York.* (1995) **T.W. Schaller. Architects: Richard Dattner Associates, Landscape Architect: Miceli Kulic.** Watercolor, 70.2cm x 93.6cm

A clearly articulated, highly detailed, and small-scale oriented graphic treatment of this proposal was selected as being most suited to a project geared toward use primarily by children.

arranged in a hierarchy appropriate to the story, which is to be told by the whole experience. The successful attempt at an expression of the elements of any given medium in service of a "greater truth" is a loose but workable definition of art.

While there will be no attempt here to delineate any absolute, objective, reality-based definition of art, this "greater truth" is often thought of as "beauty," though certainly by no means always in the strictly non-confrontational, aesthetically pleasing sense. Beauty can perhaps, in a wider definition, be thought of as order, even if that order does not necessarily please the senses. Alberti defined beauty as "a harmony of all the parts, in whatsoever subject it appears, fitted together with such proportion and connection that nothing could be added, diminished, or altered but for the worse." This lucid and definite comment confirms the satisfaction the human mind can experience while witnessing the harmonic process of perception, which begins with the general and leads to the specific. As the human mind matures, it begins to recognize and identify characteristics of the whole by unfolding the more specific elements of any number of aspects of life. Arnheim defines "diminution" as the term used by medieval musicians to articulate the process whereby "successful patterns are organized in such a way that all details are understood as elaborations" upon a central theme. This illus-

Figure 4–17. *Homeless High Rise Dwelling.* (1991) **Luis Blanc.** Wax pencil on vellum, 48.7cm x 50cm

Clearly, drawings of buildings can have a wider vocabulary than simply that of "building." "This drawing," writes Blanc, "is an illustrative comment on the effects of the last decade's building boom that left a glut of burnished, upscale, residential towers in Manhattan while subsidized housing lost 75% of its federal budget."

Figure 4–18. *Chinatown.* (1990) **Christopher Grubbs.** Pencil, 54.9cm x 42.9cm

Done largely on site shortly after the devastating San Francisco earthquake, this image captures the moonlit calm of the deserted streets with a lyrical sense of the impermanence, the fragility, and the insistence of society's claim upon Earth. The sky seems the only "positive," truly stable element of this composition, defining and supporting the light, ephemeral forms, and edges of the architecture in its timeless grasp.

trates a "hierarchic structure," writes Arnheim, "which permits the viewer or listener to grasp a complex whole as the gradual unfolding and enrichment of a theme."

The practice of architecture is, to say the least, a richly varied field which bridges realms of art and artifice and, to quote Hegel, "place and symbol." In a successful building, function and expression of form meld into, it is hoped, a seamless union. It is illustrative here to paraphrase a distinction drawn by Arnheim between "function," that which satisfies a totality of human needs, physical and emotional, and "expression," the dynamics of perception. Perceptual dynamics are concerned with less tangible, more general characteristics such as, to quote Arnheim, "openness or closedness, straightness or flexibility" which, as such, correspond more directly to characteristics of the human mind. So, in architecture, while the study of function is primarily concerned with the specifics of objects and spaces, the realm of expression is represented by more general states or ways of being. For example, consider a particular building that may be designed in such a way to skillfully eliminate windows only along its primary facade. So, because of other sources of light, the interior of this building may still function wonderfully well as a bright, well-lit, and airy space; however, the general perception of it from the street is one of darkness and foreboding. It cannot, in fairness, be said definitively in this case that the building is a "failure," but only that the "general" does not allow

Figure 4–19. *Proposal for the Battersea Power Station Development Project, London.* (1996) **James Akers. Architects: The Rockwell Group, New York.** Black prismacolor on tracing paper, 39cm x 89.8cm

So much of this firm's growing body of built projects depends upon visual excitement and the effective choice of intentional theatrical artifice. Not surprisingly, their approach to design is correspondingly organic and spontaneous. It is, therefore, to their great benefit that they regard gifted architectural visualists like Akers as indispensable members of a team—integral and essential to the very process of design.

the viewer to perceive the "specifics" accurately, and it thereby confounds a more elemental sense of harmony or beauty. The primary facade is not a proper "visual analogy" in the words of that great "romantic" rationalist, Boullee.

So much architectural artwork can be said to fail because it attempts to explicitly mimic the actual functional and tangibly physical characteristics of a building. Many of these works suggest the artist forgot that while a three-dimensional work of architecture must, by definition, stand in two worlds—the functionally specific as well as the perceptually general—a two-dimensional artwork should, by design, concern itself primarily with the expressive realm of perception. Indeed, to succeed it *must* do so.

In his *Dynamics of Architectural Form*, Arnheim quotes from Kant's *Critique of Pure Reason*, in which the philosopher describes the "architectonics of pure reason" as "the art of systems." "Under the rule of reason," writes Kant, "our cognitions must not be rhapsodic but must form a system, which alone enables them to support and promote reason's principal purposes." Later in the work Kant descibes "the rational scientific concept [as containing] the purpose and the form of the whole which is congruent to it."

Kant articulates the notion that a lucid, truly valid idea or train of thought must proceed along logical and wholly comprehensible lines to be successful. That is to say that when each element of something is inspected, it is in service to further the purpose of the whole. "All good thinking, then," concludes Arnheim, "can be said to aspire toward the condition of architecture." Following this line, superior thoughts like good buildings and good artwork are solid and well built; moreover, they are true to their initial conceptions or their "essential" inspirations. All the disparate elements of any given work of art, chosen with discretion, convene to produce an ultimate work that shines a clearer light on these separate elements; moreover, it shines a light upon the initial idea from which their existence sprang: a whole which is greater than the sum of its parts.

PART TWO

ARCHITECTURE
of the
IMAGINATION

Orpheus in Orlando. (1995) **T.W. Schaller.** Watercolor, 51cm x 76cm

Prix de Rome, Greniers Publics. (1797) **Artist/Designer: Louis-Ambroise Dubut.** Watercolor; Courtesy of École Nationale Superieure des Beaux-Arts, Paris.

This superlative piece is surprisingly representative of much of the student efforts at the École in the late 18th and early 19th centuries. The image successfully explains and illuminates its subject with equal measures of subtle interpretive skill and technical brilliance; furthermore, shades of Romanticism can be seen through the light of Rationalist formality.

Private Residence, Naples, Florida. (1995) **T.W. Schaller. Architects: Richard Meier & Partners.** Watercolor, 70.2cm x 96.3cm
Lush tropical form and color juxtaposed with tectonic formality is the essential idea of both this design scheme and the image representing it.

UNITED STATES COURTHOUSE
· FOLEY SQUARE ·

U.S. Federal Courthouse Competition, Foley Square, New York City, final design aerial view. (1994) **T.W. Schaller. Architects: Kohn Pedersen Fox and BPT Development.** Watercolor, 117cm x 156cm

Though context was an important factor, this record image of a winning design was completed as a celebration of a signature view of a realized design concept. As such, the values and color modulation in the painting were geared to showcase the new structure.

National Air and Space Museum, Washington, D.C., sectional perspective view. (1996) **T.W. Schaller. Architects: Hellmuth Obata & Kassabaum.** Watercolor, 100.2cm x 257.4cm

Since a great deal of specific information needed to be conveyed in this work, strong tones of sky and ground plane helped to establish and visually organize, in reverse silhouette, the light cool tones of the vast interior space.

LIFE Magazine, Dreamhouse. (1995) **T.W. Schaller. Architect: Dennis Wedlick.** Watercolor, 70.2cm x 70.2cm

A deeply residential effect was sought here by the use of clear, flat wash, which offset the composition to maximize pastoral landscaping elements, muted color palette, and crepuscular light of evening.

Whitehall Ferry Terminal Competition, New York City, plaza view. (1994) **T.W. Schaller. Architects: Venturi, Scott–Brown, Anderson/Schwartz-Philadelphia/NYC.** Watercolor, 61cm x 92cm

A sense of movement, activity, and access was the intention of this image, which utilizes a warm evening sky to maximize the transparency of the glazing and to complement the cool tones of the design scheme.

Proposed Plaza: Olympics 2000, Istanbul. (1994) **T.W. Schaller. Architects: Stang and Newdow Atlanta with T.W. Schaller AIA.** Watercolor, 92cm x 61cm

Though framed in both foreground and background by structure, the real focus of this piece is space—the proposed plaza in the mid-ground. The challenge was to establish the perception of great depth by value modulation and to prevent the image of the famed Hagia Sophia in the distance from overwhelming the work.

Spark Park, Houston, Texas. (1992) **Joyce Rosner. Architect: Robert Morris.** Watercolor, Calligraphy by Brody Neuenschwander, Bruges/Belgium, 51.2cm x 82cm

Objective elements of planar, elevational, and celestial information are combined by this thoughtful and skilled architect/artist to create an image of surprisingly subjective and emotive content.

LA 2015. (1987) **Artist/Designer: Syd Mead.** Gouache, 76.9cm x 51.2cm

This remarkable visualist's theatrical sense of composition and color as well as his understanding of emphasis and perspective effect by value range manipulation is displayed to great advantage in this work, intended for use by the motion picture industry.

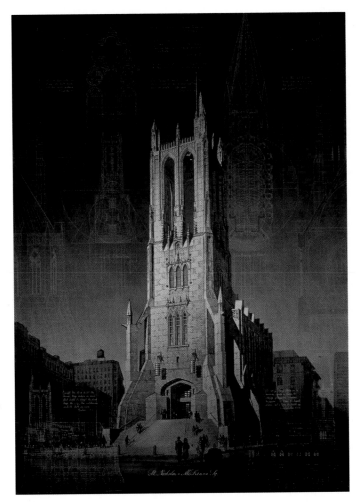

St. Nicholas, McKenna Square, New York City. (1992) **Artist/Designer: Lee Dunnette.** Ink and airbrush, 117cm x 156cm

This artist's versatility with and appropriate usage of various media is especially impressive. Notice the subtle gradations and overall sobriety of the composition and color scheme here, which was rich with information and in keeping with the sophisticated tone of the proposed subject.

Tower of Babel. (1995) **Artist/Designer: Moritoshi Nakamura.** Watercolor, 51.2cm x 76.9cm

Nakamura has achieved an inspired interpretation of the venerable "myth-of-Babel," saying much about the mutability and materiality of life and the "shifting sands" of architectural fashion.

Hans-Gert Jellen Aids Memorial. (1991) **Artist/Designer: Andy Hickes.** Mixed media and airbrush, 51.2cm x 76.9cm

In a very personal response, this artist has fashioned a moving tribute, utilizing the forms of architecture in the most directly communicative way—a framework for expression.

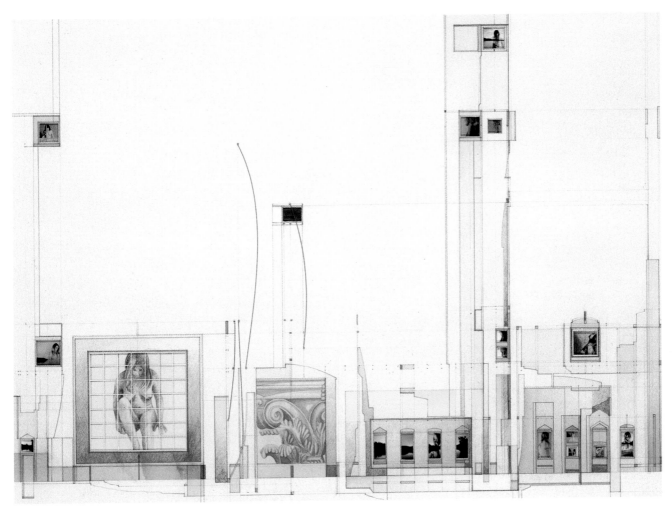

Window and Fragments: Memory and Desire. (1994) **Artist/Designer: Richard B. Ferrier FAIA.** Watercolor, graphite, metal, and photographic images, 76.9cm x 102.5cm

Done for inclusion in an invitational exhibit sponsored by the Texas Fine Arts Association, this arresting composition is a response by the prodigiously talented Ferrier, consistent with the investigative work of his ongoing *Windows and Fragments* series. This piece is, however, in keeping with the exhibit's more personal theme, using photographs as symbolic memory reference, the dialogue of architectural materiality, and compositional "negative" space to speak a unique experiential language.

Proposed Stage Set, Roman Triptych, Resphigi. (1992) **T.W. Schaller.** Watercolor, 76cm x 56cm

This image is a free adaptation and celebration of traditional Roman forms; moreover, it is a celebration of the warm Italian light which gives these forms shape and substance.

Valhalla of the Americas, Ixtapa, Mexico. (1989) **T.W. Schaller.** Watercolor, 61cm x 46cm

The cool tones of structure are silhouetted by the warm hues of atmosphere and space, the real story of this drawing.

Proposed Hydroponics Research Facility, Uruguay. (1993) **T.W. Schaller.** Watercolor, 46cm x 61cm

An effort has been made here to describe space and form by the use of pure color rather than by light/dark tonality. Warm reddish hues were assigned to the land and man-made objects, while cool green was reserved for the water and sky.

Image. (1993) **T.W. Schaller.** Watercolor, 46cm x 61cm

Inspired by the evocative photographs of New York during the 1940s by Andreas Feinenger, this image attempts to establish perceived depth by layering of atmospheric planes rather than using standard perspectival devices.

Aquasulis, Bath, England. (1993) **T.W. Schaller.** Watercolor, 93.6cm x 93.6cm

The footprint of the architecture here is established by the ancient Roman baths, but the surrounding design is an imagined future, implying both permanence and mutability. The "fixed" elements, water and sky, are treated in cooler, more "evolved" tones, while the transitory creations of man are handled in warmer, more "primal" colors.

From: The City. (1990) **T.W. Schaller.** Watercolor, 72cm x 56cm

Light is used here as a symbolic device, emanating *from* as much as being received *by* the subject building.

Proposed Archaeology Museum, Crete. (1990) **T.W. Schaller.** Watercolor, 61cm x 46cm

Time as allegory is the essential idea in this image. Perspective's implied three dimensions of height, width, and depth are augmented by a fourth-dimension—the implicit passage of the years, indicated here by the representation of progressive demateriality and by a glimpse of an expanse of infinite space.

Proposed Residential Span, Southwestern United States. (1993) **T.W. Schaller.** Watercolor, 70.2cm x 93.6cm

Few structures speak of movement as eloquently as the bridge. But to consider the span as both a means of transition *(process)* as well as a destination *(product)*, is the aim of this work. Note the visual organization of cooler blue/green tones used for all man-made horizontal elements of the natural components of sky, water, earth and vertical stone piers and the warmer coloration treatment.

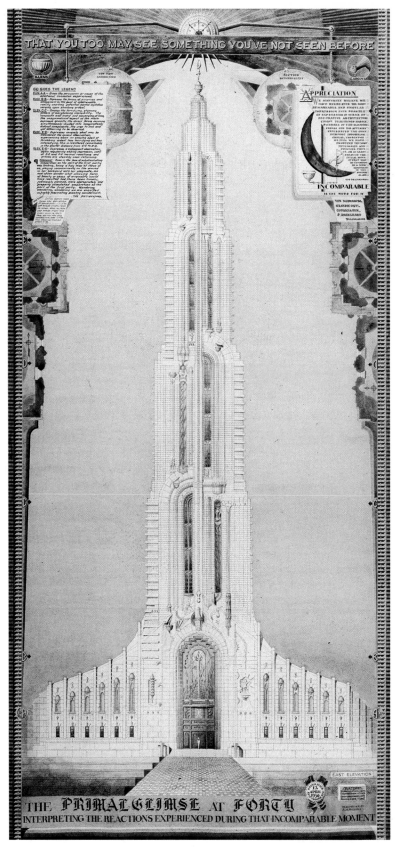

Primalglimse. (CA. 1940) **Artist/Designer: Achilles G. Rizzoli.** Colored ink, 210cm x 101cm;
Courtesy of Bonnie Grossman and The Ames Gallery, Berkeley, California.

Time and again, this artist achieved more than a response *to* or representation *of* an
inspiration—he excelled in painting inspiration itself. This strange and aptly titled
work is altogether "divine," as if having very little connection to earthly concerns
despite the implied materiality of its expressive elements.

The Architect's Dream. (1840) **Thomas Cole.** Oil on canvas, 134.6cm. x 213.5cm; Courtesy of The Toledo Museum of Art.

Cole's historical allegories were often intended, in his words, as "a higher style of landscape," divergent from his earlier pastoral or Arcadian wilderness scenes. In these later compositions, architectural elements were often employed as elements of mythic-narrative significance; embodiments of Cole's belief in the responsibility of art to respond to an elevated moral code.

Design for Die Zauberflote-The Magic Flute: Interior Court, Temple of the Sun with the Statue of Osiris, Act II Final Scene. (1816) **Artist/Designer: Karl Friedrich Schinkel.** Body color over pen and brown ink, 54.2cm x 62.5cm; Courtesy of Staatliche Museen zu Berlin.

Schinkel's monumental set designs for a new production of Mozart's 18th-century masterwork were a tremendous success. Reflecting the classical influence of Gilly, the designs (as did the music itself) explored the struggle between darkness and light. These images also reveal a remarkable sense of depth and dramatic warm/cool color shifts in an exotic neo-Egyptian format.

Cathedral of Liverpool. (1929) **Cyril Arthur Farey, (1888–1954). Architects: Sir Edwin Lutyens.** Watercolor, 80.0cm x 108.0cm; Courtesy of Metropolitan Cathedral of Christ the King, Liverpool.

One of Farey's very finest watercolor perspectives, this image succeeds in capturing both the grace and the palpable sense of strength contained in this brilliant design. The graphic results of the collaboration between two artists such as Lutyens and Farey, working at the height of their powers, are convincing in the extreme. Interestingly, the individual and collective process-oriented images of these two men are the only tangible record we have of this outstanding unbuilt design, demonstrating that architecture need not be built to be "real."

CHAPTER FIVE

Informal Process Drawing: The Sketch

The search for that which is essential in a drawing intended to convey pure emotion, for example, is not surprisingly a somewhat different process than that which may come about in the completion of drawings meant as architectural design investigations. The primary difference is to be found in the desired goal—that which is deemed essential itself. The purely emotive work of art may seek to be an actual material manifestation of feeling—joy, confu-

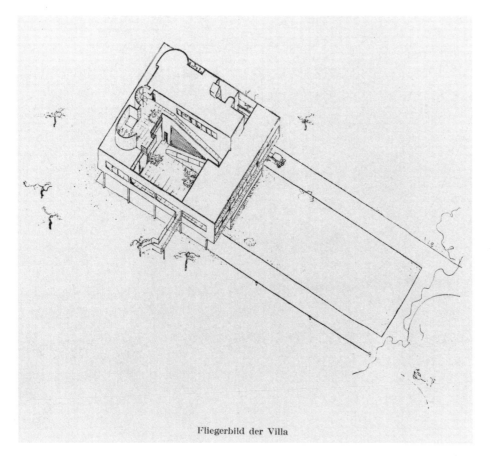

Fliegerbild der Villa

Figure 5–1. *Bird's-Eye View of Villa Savoye, from LeCorbusier and Pierre Jeannerette.* (OEURVE COMPLETE DE 1910–1929, 6TH ED. 1956) **Artist/Designer: Le Corbusier. (Charles-Edouard Jeannerette, 1887–1966).** Offset lithograph, 14.2cm x 16.0cm; Reprinted by permission of Centre d'Architecture Canadien/Canadian Centre for Architecture, Montreal.

This rather minimalist drawing from the great architect's own hand depicts one of his most legendary designs; then under construction. It is felt that Le Corbusier believed that the *concept* of a building outweighed in importance its *realization*. So his drawings often, as is the case here, preserve the strict purity of his ideas more than do the actual buildings which may have resulted.

sion, or rage—or perhaps a more metaphoric expression such as darkness or lightness, resolution or conflict, stasis or kineticism. Naturally, a work that seeks to illuminate or explore an emerging design concept is not immune to considerations of expressions such as these. Still, a concept which deals fundamentally with considerations of human habitation or utilization must, at some fundamental level, address such issues as function, site, scale, and contextuality, and no matter how optimistic the artist, it must address properties of material and atmosphere.

Nevertheless, the expressive joys of the abstract artist or the exuberant child need not be lost to the architectural designer. In fact, if a commonality is ever to be found among influential architects of the past and present, as well as among many other creative minds, it is during a project's early efforts when the artist first develops thoughts and conceptions. Most of these creative individuals quite literally, "think on paper." How similar in feeling, if not in actual content are the sketch-book noodlings of DaVinci and Frank Lloyd Wright? The energetic musical sketches of Mozart—with notes, corrections, changes, additions, and new ideas written over the page at a seemingly break-neck pace also come to mind. What is, of course, being described here, is the very nature of artistic endeavor, or its process. It is the process of inspiration or creativity itself—the act of giving face and form to the artistic impulse. The sketch, in its many guises, is the pellucid manifestation of the creative mind at work.

Figure 5–2. *Dominus Winery, California.* (1988) **Artist/Designer: I.M. Pei.** Pen on tracing paper, 58.5cm x 93.6cm; Courtesy of T.W. Schaller.

Executed in fluid line over a constructed perspective view set up, this piece succinctly shows the architect's thinking on the importance, in this specific case, of design becoming an effective amalgam of structural and site/landscape concerns.

If it is said that the creative personality is often characterized by the ability to "think with a pencil on paper," it should be understood that, in the opinion of the author, this statement, no matter how true, should not be taken too literally. That is to say, the "pencil" in question may be a pen, a paintbrush, a computer terminal's mouse, or a stick on a sandy beach. All these implements are merely a means to an end or tools to most quickly or effectively explore urgent questions at hand. Creativity and especially the *process* of creativity is not media specific. If, for example, an artist works in a watercolor medium to explore his or her ideas, the *ideas* should be the focus of the work and not the *watercolor*. Media techniques have their place, of course, but the conception is that more investigative work should be the focus and not the means by which the conception is explained or explored. It should not be assumed that this book has any "anti-digital" stance when it comes to the question of computer graphics. There is much, and there promises to be more, astoundingly investigative and viable work done by computer, both in the finished and the more conceptual vein, some examples of which are showcased between these covers. Still, as with any emerging technology, obstacles can sometimes dilute results, and *new* is not always synonymous with *better*. If, for any given artist, computer graphics prove to serve creative needs in a quicker or more satisfying manner than more "analog" devices, then, by all means, they should be explored and

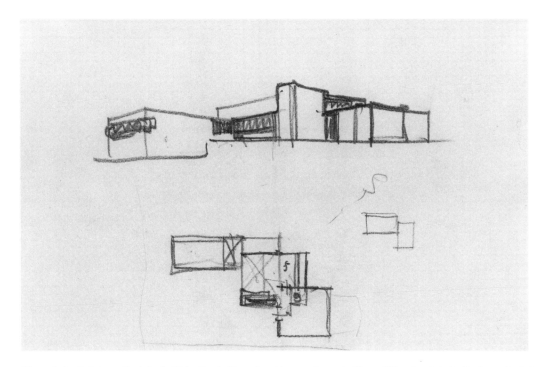

Figure 5–3. *Preliminary Sketch for the Walter Drexler House, Jena, Germany: Perspective View and Plan.* (1925) **Artist/Designer: Ludwig Mies van der Rohe (1886–1969).** Graphite on tracing paper, 20.9cm x 30.3cm; Courtesy of Centre d'Architecture Canadien/Canadian Centre for Architecture, Montreal.

Van der Rohe wrote in 1953 that architecture "depends on its time" and also that when "technology reaches its real fulfillment, it transcends into architecture." Yet, the great "artist/engineer" is concisely represented, before the computer age, in this economical, very "analog" sketch which embodies many of his recurring design precepts; for example, interlocking volumes and sliding planes—a modernist integration of object and space. It is fascinating to imagine how he might work today.

utilized to their full extent. Still, others find the simplicity and immediacy of a soft pencil and a roll of cheap paper the most expedient path to creative investigation.

Architecture, as discussed earlier, can have various meanings ranging from the study, the existence, or the production of anything from a single building to a grouping to the entire built environment. So, when discussing the topic, it is important to have a clear concensus as to the specific discipline under consideration. When a fine artist sits down to complete a work with architecture as a subject matter, the artist is generally attempting to interpret ideas about the social, aesthetic, or cultural impact of that architecture—built or unbuilt. However, when an architect draws a building, especially at an early developmental stage, it is more than likely that he or she attempts to portray ideas about actual structural, contextual, and spatial concerns.

In his fascinating and essential book, *Why Architects Draw,* Edward Robbins, anthropologist and lecturer in Urban Design at the Graduate School of Design at Harvard, explores the sometimes surprisingly varied terrain of the architectural drawing as used in modern architectural practice. He analyses the ways in which designers use drawings to explore and explain design for themselves, their colleagues, and their clients, but also the ways in which architects use drawings to establish an agenda within the social context as well, in the process of shaping our built environment for themselves in the process of design, and for their clients. For Robbins, architectural drawings can represent ideas and are useful as instruments of social practice. "Architectural drawing," he writes, "has many effects, serving as it does to join concept to its materialization and the architect as cultural creator to the architect as social practitioner. Drawing both produces architectural knowledge and is a production of that knowledge."

Robbins goes on to point out that architectural drawings are used by architects in many ways—both as representation of an object as well as an object itself. In Robbins' words, they are "the subject of conversation and the object of our endeavors."

Among the many salient points and issues raised in Robbins' book is one nearly universal fact that most architects, regardless of their aesthetic proclivities or personal and professional agendas, continue to draw as a means of exploring design. It is this area, this beautifully "grey" area between concept and reality, that the architectural drawing crosses and inhabits so perfectly and necessarily. The piece of paper that holds our thoughts in the making—that print-out, that doodle, that sketch—is the very embodiment of the creative thought process.

The pages of this chapter are devoted to these types of "process drawings"—the earliest stages of design development in graphic form. These are all drawings about something else—signposts pointing elsewhere. Understandably, and not incorrectly, the idea of the "sketch" comes to mind. While it often is a sketch—a hasty, diagrammatic, informal, kinetic, and economic piece of work—that exemplifies the process most clearly, these early stage efforts can

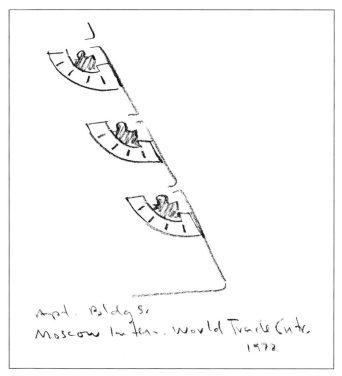

Grand Avenue—Moscow International Trade Center. (1972) Pencil, 20.5cm x 25.6cm

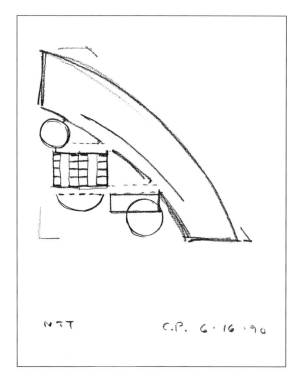

Bunker Hill Competition. (1979) Pencil, 20.5cm x 25.6cm   *NTT Plan, Tokyo.* (1990) Pencil, 20.5cm x 25.6cm

Figure 5–4. *Various Sketch Studies for a Developmental Design.* **Artist/Designer: Cesar Pelli.**

Though Mr. Pelli writes that he does not "normally work with sketches, but with models, to conceive or develop architectural direction," he does claim to have become fascinated with his drawings of this recurring and highly sculptural multi building form concept. This series of Pelli's sketches demonstrates the historic genesis of a design, the sketch used as a record of design inspiration and evolution. The concept has now been adapted to a major commission under construction; the NTT project in Tokyo, Japan, is nearing its completion.

also embrace elements of refinement and pictorialism which are not necessarily at odds with their more purely developmental nature. While the orthogonal plan, section, or elevation sketch drawing is most often what is seen on an architect's drawing board when solutions to a design problem begin to emerge, the isometric or perspective sketch is not an uncommon sight. These types of more "pictorial" representation offer excellent opportunities to explore volumetric and three-dimensional questions early on. As we saw in Arnheim's work, however, it is in the dominant horizontal and the vertical planes that human visual perception first operates and so it is often essential that a designer, regardless of which type of view is selected, first make fundamental decisions as to the figural identity, which the eventual vertical elements will describe upon the flat plane of the horizontal. In any structure intended for eventual use or habitation, it is in the horizontal plane that we can best and most easily understand the movement of people through space.

Thus, we begin to see the logic and purpose of the plan-based sketch as typically the first choice for design development drawing. Plan sketch drawings are, of course, essential to a designer in an attempt to comprehend the nature of the eventual structure at hand, but also as a means of understanding the relationship between the new structure and its context—its built or natural neighborhood of environmental influences. The contextuality of architecture is not a new concept, yet in examples of more current design and in the drawings utilized to

Figure 5–5. *Preliminary Study for the Roman Catholic Metropolitan Cathedral of Christ the King, Liverpool.* (1929) **Artist/Designer: Sir Edwin Lutyens (1869–1944).** Pencil and brown crayon on a sheet from his "virgin" pad, 13cm x 20.5cm; Courtesy of The British Architectural Library, RIBA, London.

His recurring vocabulary of a high central arch flanked by two lower arches was evident in Lutyen's direct and lively perspective drawings for this wonderful but, except for the crypt and foundation, sadly unrealized structure. Fortunately, an invaluable wealth of his process-works remains.

achieve them, a near unprecedented level of intelligence exists about the consideration of forces which make any given site adaptable and which, in turn, inform the designer as to the most "appropriate" building for that site. So, what may have been deemed as the "essential" in a developmental plan drawing of Pedersen, for example, may not be immediately apparent to the viewer; it may require some insight into the vagaries of the specific site at hand. Sun directions, sight lines, or city axes distant or even long-forgotten may all be influential to the emerging shape of both the footprint as well as the overall identity of the entire structure. A sense of tension—the conflict and potential resolution between elements—and a subsequently distinct kineticism are nearly always present in these masterly abstractions from Pedersen's office. These are qualities which are inherited by many of his finished structures, directly it seems, from these early inspirations on paper. Like all modernist expression—painting, music, and buildings—much of the message, the information, and the story of sketches such as these lies beyond the parameters of the canvas or the page. Their inspirations and the creative reaction they produce cannot be arbitrarily confined to any such classicist conceit as simple border, proportion, or resolution.

DIE SILHOUETTE DRESDENS IN GESCHNITTENEN PFLANZEN STILISIERT

Figure 5–6. *IGA Island 2003 Master Plan Competition: Blue/Green Metamorphosis, Dresden, Germany.* (1995) **Artist/Designer: James Wines,** SITE. Pen, ink, and color.

"The inspirational forces," writes Wines, "that have shaped architecture, landscape architecture and urban planning for the past eight years—and continue to influence the present—have their roots in the early Machine Age. Today . . . the most relevant sources of ideas in the building arts will be increasingly drawn from that 'ultimate machine,' the earth itself. This proposal addresses the mutable and cyclical nature of birth, death and resurrection, which defines all forms of life and specifically, this great re-emerging German city."

Figure 5–7. *Tennessee Aquarium IMAX Building, Chattanooga, Tennessee.* (1994) **Artist/Designer: James Wines, SITE.** Pen, ink, and color. Wine's enduring interest in the dialogue between the man-made and the natural—order and chaos—is reflected in the startling images of this fascinating proposal. A "building-as-a-garden" is the stated concept here—"a visual and functional microcosm of the city's most identifiable features—the river and the mountains, the materiality and scale of early waterfront industrial buildings, and certain recent architectural and urbanistic commitments that have begun to define the new regional ambience."

By their very definition, these types of "process" works are about something other than what they may be when considered simply as graphic expressions. While they may be valid and compelling artistic statements in their own right, they differ from works intended as more purely "artistic" efforts by their very "directional" nature. They are literally signposts, outlines, of another statement yet to be made. The essentials which provide the impetus for their creation are shaped and informed by the identity of an actual structure or ideas about an actual structure yet to exist; of course, it can quite rightly be said that all artwork (it is perhaps one of the definitions of art) is about something other than what is on the canvas or page itself. Still, the message or emotional impact intended by the painter or graphic artist is a direct result of the artwork itself, whereas the message or emotional impact of the architectural process drawing is generally intended to be communicated by or contained in the eventual building the drawings describe. There is of course artwork that uses architectural ideas and identities as subject matter without the intent of pointing toward or resulting in an actual structure. These works, looked at in later chapters of this book, can at times achieve levels of merit commensurate with any other expression in the realm of fine art but are, of course, not to be considered process drawing as such since their real message lies within their own artistic and intellectual parameters. Still, as hinted at earlier, process drawings may not always take the form of the scratchy, gestural economic sketch that most often may come to mind. The more "pictorial" formats such as isometric and perspective drawing (sometimes, such as in the case of their use in various architectural design competitions reaching a high level of finish) can just as likely be thought of as platforms for process explorations.

While the plan-based sketch is essential in helping to establish a projected structure's fundamental relationship to its site and its more purely functional horizontal plane identity, elevational sketches begin to give form to its more visual identity. Of course, issues such as height are easily understood in the elevational sketch, but more subjective issues such as balance, scale, and harmony can be studied in depth. It is difficult to think of the beautifully polished and refined orthogonal drawings done by students of the École des Beaux-Arts in the 19th century as "process" works, but to a great extent many of them were just that.

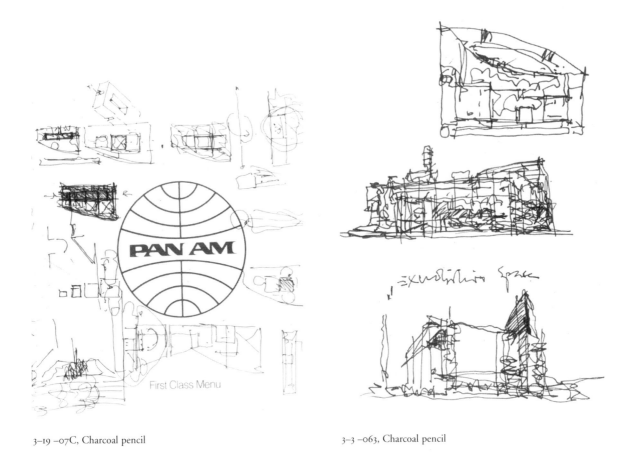

3–19 –07C, Charcoal pencil

3–3 –063, Charcoal pencil

Figure 5–8. *Tokyo International Forum Competition, Tokyo, Japan.* (1989) **Artist/Designer: Rafael Vignoly.**

From nearly four hundred entries worldwide, Rafael Vignoly's design for this project, the first ever such competition held in Japan, was selected as superior by a distinguished panel of jurors which included Pei, Maki, Tange, Gregotti, and Erickson. Some of the earliest concept impressions for his winning scheme are recorded here and expose an extraordinarily visual design imagination at work. Loose and immediate, these sketches are the very embodiment of design "process."

Though few examples of architectural artwork, of any style or in any medium before or since, can approach the meticulous finish and level of craftsmanship routinely found in so many works generated by that institution's students, it is important to remember that many of these exercises represented buildings not necessarily ever intended for construction. Rather, they were a means to another end—a student's heightened awareness and knowledge of the principles of classicism and neoclassical design that would be applied to the works of his or her later professional life. While these "studies" were commonly generated with considerations of an actual site as their basis, they were vehicles with far more validity in the general study of aesthetics and design theorem than in the interest of solving any specific building problem. Of course, unlike modernism and its subsequent disciplines which promote the idea of the possibility of unique and a near-infinite number of design solutions to almost any given problem, the classic and neoclassic ideals allowed for, if not less flexibility of expression, a much more specifically defined language of design expression parameters.

Of course, it was the established principles, with little or no differentiation between the intellectual or the aesthetic, which were the guideposts and the genesis of classicism in design. The pictorial or more strictly emotive components of architectural design were

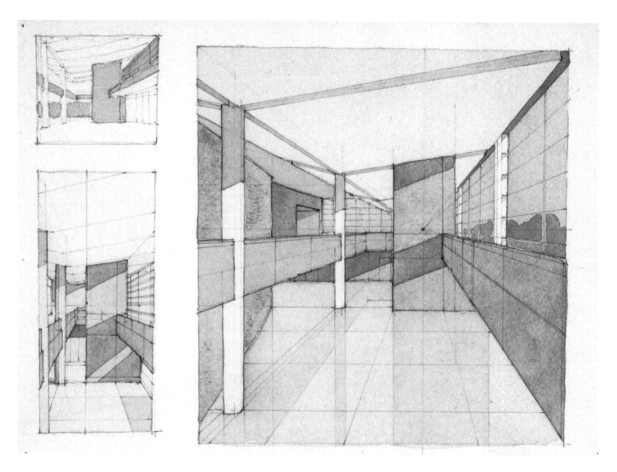

Figure 5–9. *Columbia University School of Law.* (1994) **John E. Fernandez. Architects: J.S. Polshek and Partners.** Watercolor.

Economy and directness are the key to the great effectiveness of this sketch grouping; they are a concise graphic "walk-through" of essential design elements which include volume, mass, and the effects of light.

eschewed by Beaux-Arts discipline and were largely shunned in their graphic representations as well. The use of the perspective drawing, for example, for the presentation of a formal design in competition was virtually unknown, though courses in perspective were taught at the École. As students' final designs were submitted in competition with one another for the coveted Grand Prix de Rome, the decision to have all graphics submitted in an orthogonal format had a certain logic vis-à-vis questions of clarity and equality; still, the choice had as much to do with the overall tone and belief system of classicism and the Beaux-Arts discipline in general.

So, while the rigid formality and high level of finish of so much of the student efforts done in the École des Beaux-Arts appear to discredit this work as being considered as "process" oriented, it should be remembered that all of these pieces were student design competitions, illustrative of emerging professional designers' aesthetic development. Furthermore, as we shall see, a great many pieces of architectural art, especially perhaps in the realm of design competition and often rather polished in terms of overall finish, are in fact process-

Figure 5–10. *George Mason University, Prince William Institute Biosciences Center.* (1993) **John E. Fernandez. Architects: J.S. Polshek and Partners.** Watercolor.

This image is distinguished by a valid and strikingly effective graphic treatment which simultaneously depicts both the building footprint and the perspective view.

oriented. Despite appearances, they are not so much records of a final artistic destination, but rather a documentation of one milestone of the journey.

The Age of Romanticism in the late 18th and early 19th centuries profoundly affected the ways in which almost all creative people felt about the very nature of artistic expression. The utopian spiritual purity and severity of classicism had to make room for the more secular expressions of mysticism and mortal demands of humanity. In the dominion of architectural expression, arguably no single individual had a more sweeping effect than Giovanni Battista Piranesi (1720-1778). Though he shared an interest in the forms of the ancient Greeks and Romans with proponents of the Beaux-Arts movement, Piranesi differed from that institution's belief in the unassailably utopian perfection offered by classicism. In altogether darker and more reflective depiction of the ancients, Piranesi was not afraid to illuminate the failings and mortality of these societies implying his own mortality in his emotive graphic ruminations. His interest was less in the actual forms of classicism than in the emotional power contained by these forms. His sketches of ancient ruins and his architectural fantasies are emotionally charged testimonials to the power of architectural forms and the spaces created by them. It is no surprise that he typically worked in perspective as an especially clear and direct method of pictorial and, therefore, emotional exploration. More will be made of Piranesi's impact in later chapters.

While Piranesi cannot, of course, be credited with the invention of the architectural perspective drawing—the tenets of perspective construction, having been reasonably common knowledge since the Renaissance—he must be given much recognition for his influence in establishing the emotionally and intellectually communicative power of architecture, built as well as unbuilt, as a subject of artistic expression, and as portrayed by the perspective drawing. His creative legacy is deep and can be seen as a major influence in the developing forms of literature, philosophy, and art as well as in a good deal of western architectural expression well into the 20th century. How different might the work of John Soane or Joseph Michael Gandy been, to say nothing of the American visionary Hugh Ferriss, had it not been for the potent chiaroscuros of Piranesi.

In any case, the perspective drawing became and continues to be a vital explorative tool in the architectural design process. Even those whom some may consider to be rather astringent modernists of the early 20th century were not immune to the persuasiveness of the perspective drawing in developing their work. The Russian Constructivists, Italian Futurists, the Bauhaus School, and DeStijl, for example, all employed three-dimensional images for purposes of study and presentation. Le Corbusier, Mies van der Rohe, and Frank Lloyd Wright were highly cognizant of the emotive qualities of their respective design ideas and studied them through use of the perspective sketch. Wright was especially sensitive to the

View from Street

View from Lake

Figure 5–11. *Disney Institute and Town Center Proposal, Osecola.* (1991) **T.W. Schaller. Architects: Kohn Pedersen Fox.** Watercolor and pencil, each: 28cm x 43cm

A sense of kineticism and vitality inspired both this design development and its vigorous graphic representation. "The resulting composition," wrote Pedersen of the design, "strives for an equilibrium between the whole and its diverse parts, the city and nature, collective memory and personal fantasy."

ways in which his proposals interacted, "lived," with their sites, and he believed that little was as effective a tool for exploring landscape and contextuality as was the three-dimensional visualization.

Phase 1: preliminary pencil sketch.   Phase 2: pencil sketch drawing.   Phase 3: final prismacolor drawing.

Figure 5–12. *Silver Screen Junction.* (1994) **Steve Parker. Architects: Hellmuth, Obata, & Kassabaum Sports Facilities Group, Kansas City, Missouri.** Various media, each: 25.6cm x 25.6cm

This developmental series of progress sketches by a gifted and facile architect/artist, Steve Parker, clearly demonstrates the value of hand-done drawing in the evolution of a design scheme.

Today, there are, of course, architects who still feel that perspectives are an invalid or, more to the point, a too subjective conceit. Most designers, however, see them as an invaluable avenue which offers an unparalleled opportunity to see what their proposals may *look* like and *feel* like—both at home and in context with their environments. While, as stated, some process drawings are paradoxically more, rather than less refined in overall level of finish, it is far more common and generally more appropriate that these types of exercises are gestural and suggestive in nature. As we saw in Arnheim's work, it is the tendency of perception to proceed from the general to the specific, and the most successful examples of artistic expression are often those which proceed in a lucid and natural way from the general—the concept, the big idea, the essential informing genesis—to the specific—the means and media of expression, the supporting elements, the details. It is natural to see designers or design students attempting to capture or record that "big idea" or that essential gesture of creative impulse in the quickest, most economical, and pure fashion—the sketch. These documents are useful as early design stage devices for client presentations, but are typically even more valuable as building blocks of an evolving design—veritable snapshots of process.

Naturally, designers who trust in the power of the perspective visualization and are reasonably facile with a pen or pencil often develop such sketches themselves as an organic element of their own creative thought processes. Still, others employ the services of a skilled staff member to graphically explore design ideas in tandem.

Other times, a freelance perspectivist may be called upon to visually and literally record various steps along the path toward a finalized design. These drawings can range in scope from the extremely vigorous and gestural types of work, completed in an hour or less, to more refined sketches, requiring a day or more to complete. In these cases, the freelance perspectivist may act as a literal "hired-gun" traveling to the office of the designer to work alongside him or her. In many such cases, the perspectivist may act as an indispensable element of a larger design team turning out any number of quick sketches in an attempt to *develop* as much as to *record* an emerging concept. Since a good many professional architectural illustrators are also architects and gifted designers in their own right, it is often the wise architect, whose time is short or whose graphic skills may be less developed, who may avail him- or herself of the talents of these individuals. Still, the assertion that the design architect who has at least a modicum of facility with a sketch pencil stands in much better stead of producing a visually harmonious or successful design than the one who does not, must surely bear some significant element of truth. Almost every design will appear in a graphic format at some point prior to its eventual construction, and so it stands to reason that a degree of comfort with and strength in graphic visualization cannot help but fortify the validity of the final design.

The Lagoon

River Concert

A Winter Garden

Figure 5–13. *Three Manhattan Waterfront Views: New York Waterfront Competition, The Municipal Art Society, New York City.* (1987) **Artist/Designer: Richard Lovelace.** Charcoal on tracing paper, each: 20.5cm x 25.6cm

These views perfectly illustrate the need of the image used in a design competition to impart a story boldly and with utmost impact; the tale here, told primarily by a masterful control of the effects of light, is as much about the proposal's contextual impact and emotive effect as about any design specifics. It is a powerful and economic interpretation of form and space.

It's important here to understand the nature of the successful sketch or process drawing as compared with artwork which represents a completed or finalized design. Of course, there are similarities, and at times one cannot distinguish one type of work from another, but there remain crucial distinctions. The formal presentation drawing, representing a structure whose every design detail has been formalized and whose use is more one of record or for purposes of marketing, is, by its very nature, far more about *product* than it is about *process*. It may or may not be viewed as sufficiently "artistic" depending on how well the artist conveyed the hierarchy of elements, how clearly the essential is preserved and delineated, and how the whole is orchestrated. Still, the formal presentation drawing nearly always contains a far more emphatic insistence upon specifics and detail which can, if the artist is not sufficiently vigilant, dilute or even obfuscate entirely the essential artistic gesture of the structure and of the artwork. Rightly, a client needs to know, for example, exactly how many floors are being proposed, how many and what type of windows are being paid for, or specifically, what the nature of the building materials may be. So, more often than not, the required details are allowed to dominate the work and dictate the nature of the drawing at hand. However, the client needs, or should need, to know something more.

The directness and relative simplicity of the architectural sketch can almost assure the alert and skilled artist of success. Toward that end, a simple maxim might be: "Identify the essential and preserve it." That essential, as we have seen, may be a shape, a relationship, a directionality, or an effect of light. If this one primal element is clearly stated and all other elements of the drawing fall into line behind it, a compelling work of art will almost always result. In more process-oriented work, it is nearly impossible and imprudent to portray details and specifics of wall surfaces or materiality that have yet to be defined. A judicious use of the representation of specific design detail is a characteristic quality of the most notable sketch works. Sometimes, a line or two, a gesture, a color, or a shape are all that may be needed to tell the essential story at hand.

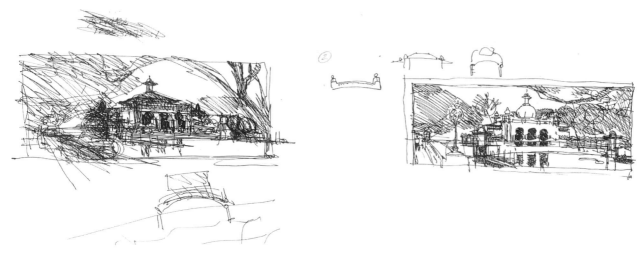

a

b

c

d

e

Figure 5–14. *Merang Laguna Resorts, Malaysia.* (1996) **Christopher Grubbs. Architects and Planners: Wimberly Allison Tong & Goo, Honolulu, Hawaii.** Ink on paper, a and b: 11.7cm x 27.3cm; c, d, and e: 15.6cm x 40.95cm

In this fascinating series of lucid and accomplished sketches, we not only see a representation of process, but we can truly see process itself. We see a design evolving in perspective, evolving at home in its site, and before our eyes. Though undeniably more skilled than many, this artist/designer offers a most convincing argument for this book's major premise; that there is really very little substitute for the designer who can "think on paper."

Media is, of course, important in these kinds of works; still, more important is the manner in which the media of choice is employed. So, while airbrush or computer imaging may appear to be more suited to the formal presentation, it could be used in a decidedly more gestural or economic fashion. Watercolor—opaque or transparent—is equally at home in either formal or informal applications. The same can be said of pen and ink or pencil— either graphite or color. Nevertheless, because of its speed of application and fluidity, transparent watercolor lends itself most naturally to sketch work, especially when any suggestion of tone, color, and the effects of light is required. Watercolor may be superseded only by use of the soft graphite pencil at the front line of sketch production. Capable of producing line or tone with almost equal dispatch, the pencil is quite simply unsurpassed at providing an unfettered channel from the creative mind directly onto the paper. In many ways, it is the very symbol of process.

CHAPTER SIX

The "Finished" Process Drawing

In the previous chapter, we looked at the ways in which process drawings differ from more finished work—not so much in technique or finish of media application as in fundamental intent. In this chapter, the finished work is thought of less as artwork that attains a high degree of sophisticated technical expertise and more as pieces which record a destination rather than a journey—the end of Process, not the process itself. It is the purpose and design of the process drawing to record a step on the way to somewhere else. The informal sketch work may be the best and most appropriate method to record this process, but, as exemplified by architectural design competition drawings, clearly it is not the only way to perceive these images.

Figure 6–1. *The Chicago Tribune Building.* (1925) **Hugh Ferriss. Architects: Howells and Hood.** Charcoal crayon on board, 36.8cm x 31.1cm; Courtesy of Avery Architectural and Fine Arts Library, Columbia University in the City of New York.

In 1922, *The Chicago Tribune* sponsored a design competition whose objective was to "secure for Chicago the most beautiful office building in the world." Arguably the most significant architectural competition in history resulted in nearly three hundred entries worldwide and a wealth of "paper" architecture, many examples of which resonate to this day. The magnificent design which emerged as victor remains among the world's great buildings but no less impressive is this drawing completed by Ferriss some years later in which light both dissolves and eludes form. Rather than seen, the building's presence is truly felt.

Design competitions may assume a variety of forms ranging from the small-scale and informal in-house exercise at a design office to the massive, far-reaching, and very public international event. Examples of the latter may involve a great number of high-profile design firms willing to commit large quantities of manpower, time, and money to vie for a winning place. Of course, a first-place win is the ultimate desire of most entrants in such endeavors, but still, in the case of highly visible and widely publicized competitions for notable civic buildings or environments, the notoriety gained by something less than a first-place finish can have nearly as desirable an effect in terms of publicity—especially in the case of gifted, emerging, and less well-known firms. So, while few designers sacrifice their time to enter cost intensive competitions hoping *not* to win, benefits can be derived by other than first-place finishers. With this in mind, it should not be surprising to discover that not all buildings designed for very site-specific competitions are actually intended to be realized, at least not in the precise form in which they are portrayed. Even in the case of winning entries, it is not unusual to find the resultant commissioned and constructed building to differ significantly from that which is represented in the submitted competition graphics. Competition entries often represent an "extreme" solution to the proffered design problem. Construction budget guidelines could be threatened; site coverage or height restrictions, for instance, could be pushed beyond suggested limitations. None of this is to suggest that most architects are necessarily errant or rebellious by nature, only that they may wish to show their "optimum" design solution. At best, they may hope that the seductiveness of their solution will convince the jury that their entry is not

Figure 6–2. *Chicago Tribune Competition.* (1922) **Artist/Designer: Harold R. Zook (1890–1949).** Ink and wash on paper, 151cm x 73.5cm; Courtesy of The Art Institute of Chicago, Gift of Robert H. Reingold through a prior gift of the Three Oaks Wrecking Company.

Chicago architect Zook submitted this earnest but unsuccessful design to the competition which, if nothing else, displays the high level of design scholarship and draftsmanship that was once the norm.

Figure 6–3. *The Royal Exchange, London.* (1840) **Artist/Designer: Charles Robert Cockerell (1788–1863).** Pen, pencil, and sepia wash, 68.6cm x 127cm; Courtesy of The British Architectural Library, RIBA, London.

Cockerell, along with Alfred Waterhouse, may well best personify the type of "old school" architect/artists whose design and graphic abilities evolved from and sustained one another. In Cockerell's beautiful perspective of an unexecuted competition design, it is truly difficult to determine with which skill he displayed more facility.

only superior, but possibly even worthy of having various parameters stretched to accommodate its obvious brilliance! More likely, it is wished that the submitted design will sufficiently impress and convince a jury to have no alternative but to select them as the designers of the "real" building. In this sense, it can be seen that the graphics used to "sell" this design, no matter how refined, are at heart process works because they represent another step—albeit a more evolved step than an earlier design stage sketch—along the path to a final design solution.

Ultimately, a competition drawing must *sell!* Certainly, to a large extent, all architectural drawing can be seen as an attempt to sell something—an idea, an approach, an actual building, or the capabilities of a specific designer. But unlike drawings done for marketing or other more specifically commercial concerns, which by and large attempt to sell the public on the very specific merits of an actual building, the architectural design competition drawing has an additionally different task. It attempts to sell an often very discerning jury, in the face of potentially formidable rivals, on the merits of a specific design firm or, more commonly, a design firm/developer team. It is often reputation, ability, and skill that are being sold as much as the intricacies of any actual design solution. That being said, the graphics utilized by the design/development team are often of utmost importance in convincing the jury of their professional merits as well as the strengths of their submitted design. The drawings must be capable of both gaining and maintaining attention as well as in quickly and clearly imparting information. Subtleties of execution and content, which may give more contemplative works their appeal, may have little or no place here. Often, the artist must be capable of implying specificity and glossing over unnecessary or unresolved details. Giving

Figure 6–4. *Whitehall Terminal Competition.* (1994) **Lee Dunnette. Architects: Hardy Holzman Pfeiffer.** Mixed media.

Again, this most gifted artist proves that the appropriate handling of any given medium is the key to an image's success. Thus, in this view, we know that a kinetic, bustling terminal is more than just a building; it is an atmosphere, it is an experience.

the appropriate amount of graphic information is crucial; for example, too much information and the overall gesture, the essential idea, may become weakened or diffuse. Likewise, too little graphical information may imply a lack of design consideration, or confidence, and a hesitant, unresolved, or insubstantial pall may descend on the work.

Though it is often the case that informal sketch-based perspective drawings are completed for design competitions, it is more common to see larger works of greater ambition and technical complexity submitted, especially for competitions with a high public or professional profile. While similarities between successful examples of these more and less complex works are not apparent at first glance, they do appear upon reflection. Their commonality lies not so much in their relative levels of *content* as in their consistency of *intent.* The story they have to tell illustrates a hierarchy of creative design impulses and reactions. What they have to sell is the essential idea—the central informing design gesture of the piece. Despite a higher level of finish or greater amount of detail, the successful architectural design competition drawing should be able to tell its tale with the same immediacy and clarity as the quick and economical sketch.

While contradictory or at the very least paradoxical, the formal competition drawings completed at the École des Beaux-Arts discussed earlier conveys many examples of successful process-oriented graphic storytelling. Certainly, few examples of these magnificent and luminous works can be accused of being "economical" or lacking in detail or finish. But it should be remembered that detail—or to be more specific, the harmonic and proportionate resolu-

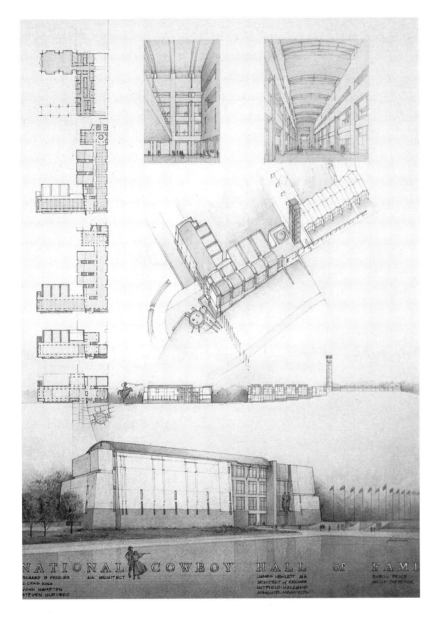

Figure 6–5. *National Cowboy Hall of Fame Addition Competition.* (1992) **Richard B. Ferrier FAIA. Architects: FIRM X; Ferrier, Hampton, Quevedo and King; James Hewlet.** Watercolor and graphite, 70.2cm x 93.6cm

A wealth of design information is accessed by clever and skillfully done composite views such as this which was completed by all members of the Firm and received an AIA Dallas Design Award in 1992.

tion of that detail by the play of light upon surface—is the central idea of much Beaux-Arts architectural design, especially as portrayed in the rendered elevation format. The more graphically refined, defined, and clearly delineated works stood a far better chance of success than did their less well-resolved competitors. These works illuminated their author's talent, skill, erudition, and promise far more than they may have showcased any specific building intended for construction. In this light, the dogmatics presumed to be inherent in the aesthetic of Beaux-Art design are, in fact, tempered with the knowledge of a surprising degree of subtle, abstract, and understated artistic expressiveness.

The formal design competition drawing is an ideal platform for the production of process-based artwork, which is among the most expressive and effective one could hope to find in the architectural idiom, but it is far from the only basis. As we have seen, the sketch-based drawing used to present an initial design idea can certainly result in a dramatic and compelling image. In truth, architecture or architectural ideas and concepts can provide the

(above) **Figure 6–6.** *U.S. Federal Courthouse Competition, Foley Square, New York, view from Foley Square.* (1993) **T.W. Schaller. Architects: Kohn Pedersen Fox.** Watercolor, 117cm x 156cm

The graphic representation of the important and distinguished foreground buildings was subdued in an effort to focus attention upon the more distant tower—the focus of the piece.

(right) **Figure 6–7.** *U.S. Federal Office Building Competition, Foley Square, New York, aerial view.* (1993) **T.W. Schaller. Architects: Kohn Pedersen Fox.** Watercolor, 117cm x 156cm

Contextual identity was the clear directive of this graphic response.

genesis for process-oriented artwork of enormously varied subject matter and use requirements. From editorial, sales, and advertising pieces to posters, matte painting, and production design concepts for film and stage work, architecture and the elements of architecture, are used to great effect.

Architectural artwork, commissioned for presentation or marketing purposes, is perhaps the most familiar or frequently seen of such work. The presentation drawing's task is to convince a specifically targeted audience—town or city officials, specific demographic consumers, or the public in general—of the merits of an established or already constructed design. Typically far different in approach than the often more dramatic and expressive

Figure 6–8. *Miyagi Arena.* (1990) **Hideo Shirai. Patron: Taisei Corporation.** Airbrush, pen, and ink, 41cm x 61.5cm

Any suggestion of the media of airbrush as being coldly static or overly technical is dispelled by the skillful modeling of light effects in this highly dramatic representation which demonstrates that it is the *artist*, not the *medium*, who controls expression.

design competition work, these pieces, if skillfully done, can achieve a certain high level of artistic integrity if, as touched upon earlier, they succeed in maintaining an appropriate hierarchy of elements. The level of detail, no matter how extensive, can still be made to answer and not to dictate the primary aesthetic gesture of the piece.

As clarification, it should be said that even in the cases where these drawings may explicitly reflect the design of a building as it is or will be built, these drawings still, in context, act as process pieces. The reason for this is found in their functionality—the fact that they all point toward another creative, yet directly commercial end. These works of art exist in the express service to another form of expression. Of course, this distinction is not drawn as any attempt to diminish their potential impact as autonomous artistic statements in their own right, but by way of gaining a fuller view of their governing contexts, and thereby, a deeper understanding of the aesthetic impulses and choices which framed and informed their creations. As an added note, artwork created by the artist expressly for sale should not be viewed as "process-oriented" even though it may have a commercial component; it is essentially an income for the artist. In this discussion, "artistic motivations" within the creation of a particular work should not be confused with the external "motivations of an artist."

As touched upon earlier, architectural competitions or, for that matter, presentation or marketing concerns are not the only venues that allow for the execution of process-based

KUALA LUMPUR
CITY CENTRE

Figure 6–9. *Proposed City Center Competition, Kuala Lumpur.* (1993) **T.W. Schaller. Architects: Kohn Pedersen Fox.** Watercolor, 76cm x 56cm

Despite any appearance of "completeness," a simple arrangement of sculptural forms modeled by or against a strong sky was the intent in this more "finished," process-oriented work.

Figure 6–10. *Saitama Arts Theatre, Sectional Perspective View.* (1994) **Moritoshi Nakamura. Architects: Hisao Koyama Atielier, Tokyo.** Watercolor, 51.2cm x 76.9cm

A tremendously skilled artist, Tokyo-based Nakamura has blended a modern interpretation of formal Beaux-Arts sensibility with a graphic theatricality perfectly suited to the nature of this proposal.

architectural artwork. Interests with decidedly non-architectural goals as their ultimate aim can frequently employ the forms of architecture in graphics and production. These forms are often used as non-verbal representatives of individual or societal states and attitudes or, more simply, as highly effective at establishing a desired mood or atmosphere.

Avid fans of cinema, especially films of the science fiction genre, will find it difficult to forget such classics as Fritz Lang's *Metropolis* from 1926 and the 1936 filming of the H.G. Wells' tale, *Things to Come*, which articulate portentous futuristic visions and, in the case of the latter film, the successes and failures of an entirely glass-based society. Aside from sporadically compelling storylines and advanced production values for their time, what distinguishes these utopian fantasies is their overriding architectural sensibility. Architectural forms, concepts, and images are used as a metaphor for progress and as symbols of advanced civilization, both in the positive and the negative sense. Stills from both of these films reveal compositions of intense drama and strength, which make it clear that the forms of structure, represented graphically, can assume great emotional weight, and thereby, they can speak of far more than merely construction elements. They can often speak, quite literally, for characters who won't or don't speak for themselves.

Figure 6–11. *American Embassy, Moscow.* (1995) **T.W. Schaller. Architects: Hellmuth Obata & Kassabaum.** Watercolor, 93.6cm x 93.6cm

Light, cool tones were used to identify a large proposed glass addition, contrasted against the more earthy tones of the existing structure, to explain the design intent and to influence viewer opinion. An effort was made in this image to create a palpable "transparency" to symbolize political transition to a "new order"—a post Cold-War sense of accessibility.

Though more often perhaps, in such works, it is the image of the "City" that speaks its Orwellian text most eloquently. In these early film projects and others like them, the idea of the futuristic, "ideal" city is expressed in overall production design, primarily by the graphic use of matte or scene painting, that is expected to carry, to symbolize, the myth of the "Future." As a creation of man, the image these early modernists had of the city were not unlike imagery in the myth of Babel for Medieval civilizations—an irresistible appeal. The city symbolized the best and the worst aspects of man's insatiable arrogance and ambition— hope and despair at once.

More modern examples in the field also contain any number of striking and powerful examples of production design and still imagery. Such films as Terry Gilliam's *Brazil*, the *Alien* series, or Ridley Scott's *Blade Runner* from 1982 exhibit far more than just the inter-mittent riveting still shot. Like the pioneering earlier films they also utilize in tandem with much advanced movie-making technology, the forms and language of architecture are used to establish an overall mood or atmosphere. Still, they do provide astonishing stills as wit-nessed, for instance, by the work of contemporary artists such as Syd Mead on the afore-mentioned *Blade Runner*.

Aside from the rather Gothic gloom of many examples of the futuristic fantasy genre, other films display, in a sometimes less bombastic manner, an essentially "architectural" nature or sensibility. The films are far less dependant upon the completely painted flats, char-

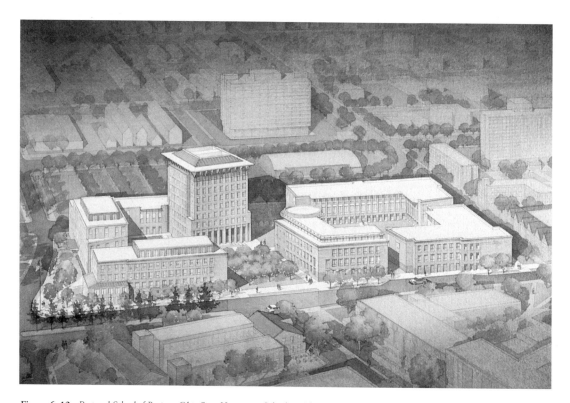

Figure 6–12. *Proposed School of Business, Ohio State University, Columbus, Ohio.* (1995) **T.W. Schaller. Cooper Robertson and Partners/ Kallman McKinnell and Wood.** Watercolor, 78cm x 117cm

To create a coherent sense of unity among the diverse elements of this scheme in an active university setting, a care-ful modeling of dark and light, warm and cool values was achieved by means of large graded washes of spectral color.

140

acteristic of largely studio-bound efforts from the 1920s or 1930s, since technical advancements allow modern films the ability to create a mobile, all-encompassing atmosphere in production design. In this regard, the film work of Britain's Peter Greenaway and Derek Jarman come immediately to mind. In Greenaway's *Draughtsman's Contract* from 1982 (an odd, although compelling, mixture of architectural drawing and sex), and in his *Belly of an Architect* from 1993, or in Jarman's 1986 film *Caravaggio,* we see characters straining against, or rather within, environments of intentional architectural theatricality. The production designs for interior or exterior shots act as rooms, as containers, for the dramas unfolding within. It should be noted too that in each of the examples the character's struggle for or against *containment,* personal and/or societal, appears to be the essential, primary theme of the screenplay. Also, in still after still of these films, we see shots aligned with intentional use of one-point perspective, symmetries played against asymmetries, and scenes illuminated with purposefully "unnatural" lighting effects. Traces of Piranesian hyperbole are noted here as well as a sort of post-modernist Romanticism but primarily an updated homage to a grand history of theatrical stage design, dating at least as far back as the Baroque. At the very least, these films make a strong case for the communicative power of architectural forms.

Surely, the world of stage design has also provided endless memorable imagery—both in the case of design concept drawings and the "architectural" environments they help to create onstage. Modern stage designers Ian MacNeil and John Lee Beaty have created some of the few effective environments achieved in recent years. Beaty's recent efforts for a revival of *The Heiress* were overwhelmingly "architectural." Based on the novel *Washington Square* by Henry James, the play traces the events and non-events of a wealthy young woman's life who is trapped and repressed by her Victorian-era society and domineering father. The architecture

View by Day

View by Night

Figure 6–13. *Friedrichstadt Passagen, Berlin.* (1995) **T.W. Schaller. Architects: Pei Cobb Freed.** Watercolor, each: 93.6cm x 100.2cm

The proposed uses of this project were judged to have equally critical merit by both day and night; therefore, two images, from identical points of view, were completed with appropriately divergent lighting effects to help underscore the point.

of the set, which represented a single room of the house with subtly transparent walls, succeeded in capturing a sense of the oppressive order and containment of the life within, as well as the vague notion of the knowledge of "something else" beyond.

In the field of operatic stage design, architectural sensibility and theatricality are completely at home. New York City's Metropolitan Opera has produced many such examples

Figure 6–14. *Whitehall Ferry Terminal Competition, New York, Plaza view.* (1994) **T.W. Schaller. Architects: Rafael Vignoly.** Watercolor, 61cm x 92cm

The primary design statement here is the brilliant design concept whose signature roof form literally speaks the language of movement.

Figure 6–15. *Whitehall Ferry Terminal Competition, New York, waterside view.* (1994) **T.W. Schaller. Architects: Venturi, Scott-Brown, Anderson/Schwartz, Philadelphia/NYC.** Watercolor, 78cm x 117cm

A dramatic, late-evening view was selected as the most effective way of telling the story of this proposal. The project was intended as a major center of travel informed by the great clock which symbolized time.

over the years—Philip Glass' *The Voyage* and Puccini's *Tosca* to name but two. In its sparse modernism, the design for the Glass work by Robert Israel is in direct contrast to the more baroque opulence of Franco Zeffirelli's sets for the Puccini's work, but both succeed in providing architectural environments of stunning power. Moreover, both productions select essential visual themes which are perfectly appropriate to the nature and historical context of the musical narratives unfolding on the stage.

Not unlike the gestural sketch-based drawing, media choice in the completion of more formal, finished works, regardless of their use, is far less important an issue than are decisions about specific media application. Anything from pen and ink to digital imaging can be a valid approach. Still, to some degree, a cleaner, more lucid application is generally what is called for as an appropriate response to the essential design gesture. For example, where a single shape or sense of directionality is the militating factor in a more early-stage process sketch, an overall atmosphere, quality of light, or convincing sense of place more likely dictates the piece that is more complex or highly resolved. So, while a few brisk charcoal or pencil strokes suffice perfectly for the former, a more considered and deliberate application of tones and colors is required for the latter. The question is one of appropriateness. In perspective interpretations of proposed structures or environments, it is always, to some degree, the idea of light that controls the hand of the artist. Yet, this idea takes on a distinctly different meaning when, as is often the case in set design, a convincing sense of light is determined to be the one essential idea of the piece. Consequently, the results are markedly diverse when this idea is used to complete a sketch or a more formal work.

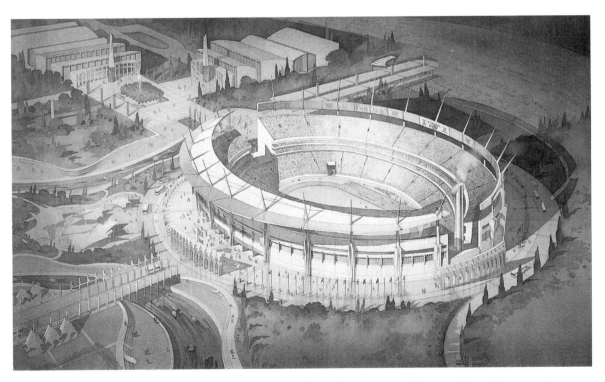

Figure 6–16. *Proposed Stadium, Olympics 2000, Istanbul.* (1994) **T.W. Schaller. Architects: Stang and Newdow, Atlanta.** Watercolor, 61cm x 92cm
A careful modeling of light and value ranges by washes of spectral color was employed to heighten the sense of information and drama in this composition of large-scale structures.

In the instances just cited, media application becomes a more critical issue. As color, while it could well be, is often not part of the equation in the sketch drawing, tone and shape take on increased significance. If color in the more formal work must carry added communicative weight, its application becomes just that much more important. Notice the ways in which light and color carry a simultaneous message, or rather, how color becomes the framework, the medium, by which light most effectively tells the essential story. In these cases, more fluid, transparent color, capable of a wide tonal modulation, is generally the wisest or most expedient and appropriate choice. Transparent watercolor, applied in clean controlled washes, is one highly effective way of achieving this end; though in fairness, similar effects may be achieved in any number of other mediums. The somewhat more obvious point is that while subtle or intricate effects require a certain brand of media application, the bold, gestural type of work also demands an appropriate media and media application response. Beyond this, however, the artist should come to an awareness as to the approach most suited to the work at hand from the outset of the completion of a piece. Copious amounts of perfectly delineated detail would be incongruous on a drawing designed from inception as a sketch. Conversely, very sketchy or gestural elements may feel ill at ease in the more formal presentation piece.

Finally, in a work that at any level of detail is intended to carry dramatic weight, it is not uncommon to see a certain degree of dramatic hyperbole employed to help direct the

Figure 6–17. *Proposed U.S. Ambassador's Residence, Kuwait.* (1994) **T.W. Schaller. Architects: RTKL/Washington.** Watercolor 93.6cm x 100.2cm

Issues of climate and atmosphere most clearly informed both design and graphic representational decisions.

144

perception of viewer and emphasize the chosen essential idea. In fact, it is a device the artist would be well-advised to investigate. This kind of "exaggeration for effect" is most at home in works intended to illustrate ideas for the theater or the cinema, but it should not be overlooked as a perfectly legitimate device for enhancing the communicative effectiveness of more strictly "architectural" presentation or commercial drawings.

By way of example, it is not necessarily suggested that the actual proportions or relative size of spaces or objects should be changed in any given drawing. However, if for instance, it is a sense of height that is deemed to be the most crucial aspect of a design, a dominance of vertical lines in a pen and ink or pencil work will help to establish this concept clearly in the viewer's mind. The sense of daylight flooding into an interior space can be enhanced by pushing illuminated areas to their graphic extreme. Furthermore, in color work, the selection of warm rather than cool tonalities for sunlit spaces can subtly suggest the feeling of the sun's heat. Also, the overall tones in a painting or drawing can be orchestrated to focus attention on especially important areas or, conversely, detract from or gloss over other less critical ones, by increasing the level of contrast in the focus area and decreasing it in others. Furthermore, one can increase the overall level of contrast between an entire area of interest and the rest of the drawing or painting. This "silhouette" technique is particularly effective in many media at various levels of finish and can work in either direction. That is to say, the entire focus,

Figure 6–18. *Pattana Building, Bangkok.* (1994) **T.W. Schaller. Architects: Pei Cobb Freed & Partners.** Watercolor, 70.2cm x 93.6cm
This vignette view of a mid design-stage proposal helped designers study the sometimes difficult interface of tower, base, and groundplane.

space or building, can be made to appear considerably darker against a light surround or, conversely, far lighter within an overall darker work.

Another effective technique, often to be used in conjunction with silhouetting in color work, is the use of "temperature" variations. For example, a proposed structure, space, or environment graphically portrayed largely in light, warm tones and set into a context or atmosphere of primarily darker, cool tones will often have a considerably greater visual impact than if the entire work were completed in a single overall warm or cool range of colors and values. Naturally, the reverse condition, a generally cool focus in a warm surround, will have an equally strong effect though it may hold a different emotional impact. In general, cooler, darker tones are felt as being more "sober," more settled, or more resolved than the vibrant, "vital" range of warm tonalities. One is reminded here of cinematographer Storaro and his theories of color response.

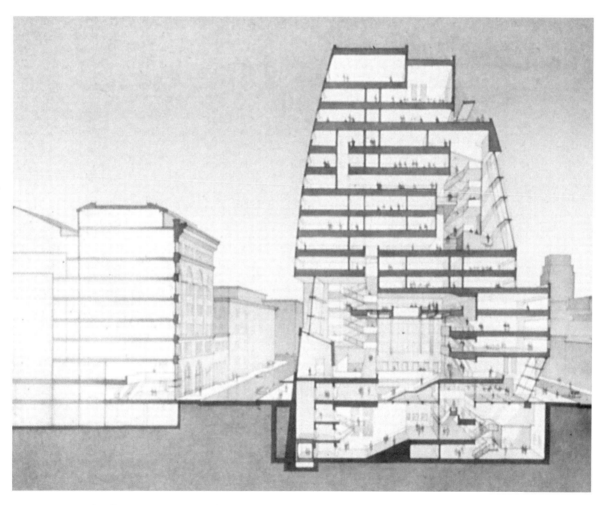

Figure 6–19. *Baruch College, New York City, sectional perspective view.* (1996) **T.W. Schaller. Architects: Kohn Pedersen Fox.** Watercolor, 96.3cm x 102cm

This rather academic choice of view seemed the most propitious in an attempt to graphically explain the large and interconnected system of atria as well as to address concerns of function and scale.

Overall values in a work of art can be modulated in both black-and-white and color work as well. A dark line, shape, or area can be used to help explain or emphasize an expanse of light just as a lighter element can take a supporting role for a more critical darker zone. Certainly, it is no surprise to find that the overall darkness or lightness of a work can be used to manipulate and exaggerate an emotional response in the viewer. So, in drawings of buildings which are intended to impart a sober or authoritative public face, such as certain municipal or governmental structures, a slightly darker or more subdued overall palette and tonal range are more appropriate. But in works that are used to explain residential or retail-oriented designs or spaces, brighter, sunnier colors and a wider range of value and hue is more in keeping with the essence of these subjects. In both examples, the desired "direction" of the value range, as well as the selected color range, can be emphasized by slightly pushing, or "bumping up," the appropriate tones and hues to more strongly make the essential point of the story.

The few types and specific examples of drawings cited in this chapter, regardless of their use, of their level of finish, or of their validity as works of art in their own right, have something more in common. They are all, to a greater or lesser extent, about something else. They all serve to guide the viewer to another level of perception or experience. While it can be said, with justification, that all art is, to some degree, about something else, these are specifically pieces that support, explain, or supplement another art form. It should not, however, be assumed that such "art about art" is by necessity any less valid or "real" than artwork completed primarily as an autonomous "product." While these pieces may by design point to another destination, many provide highly satisfying and "complete" detours and destinations as well.

CHAPTER SEVEN

The Black Sun of Piranesi

In her remarkable and insightful essay, "The Dark Brain of Piranesi," Marguerite Yourcenar discusses the influences and impact of this unique visionary. Succinctly, she describes some of his early artistic impressions as being distinguished from fashionable drawings of the day by "their intensity, their strangeness, their violence—as if struck by the rays of a black sun." The inherent contradiction in that poetic phrase only serves to underscore a number of paradoxical elements of the life and work of this complex genius.

Born in 1720, Giovanni Battista Piranesi, called by biographer and Piranesi scholar John Wilton-Ely "The most Roman of artists," was Venetian at heart, having spent the first 20 years of life in that great artistic and cultural center. Visiting Rome only once for an

Figure 7–1. *Architectural Fantasy.* (CA.1741–1744) **Giovanni Battista Piranesi.** Pen, brown ink, and brown wash, 32.9cm x 49.1cm; Courtesy of The Pierpont Morgan Library, New York; Gift of Janos Scholz, 1974.27

In contrast to his more polished print work, Piranesi's sketches on paper—like this example from his stay in Rome—reveal his artistic temperament at its most exuberant and inventive.

extended period that began in 1740, he came to be praised by many as emblematic of, and singularly instrumental in, the dawning of the age of Romanticism. His prolific outpourings of work were represented primarily by his etchings, contained in *Prima Parte di Architetture e Prospettive* from 1743 and in *Invenzioni Capricci di Carceri* from about 1745, as well as by hundreds of plates of topographical views, or *vedutista*, of Roman antiquity. The publications represented architectural fantasies, *capricci*, based upon purely fictive structures—most notably *carceri*, prison structures. Though not completely unappreciated in his own day, not unlike the work of many supremely gifted artists, Piranesi's visions were sufficiently ahead of his time to have their full import only gradually perceived, long after his death in 1778.

The son of a stonemason and nephew of a prominent architect, Piranesi continued through his life to practice as and consider himself, at heart, an architect and builder. However, it is surely his unbuilt and, more to the point, his *unbuildable* structures upon the two-dimensional page that have most profoundly shaped both his career and his legacy. Writer Robert Harbison terms him, "one of the most persuasive paper architects" from whom "many have learned that they prefer shams to the truth . . ." Yet, the potential veracity of such a statement notwithstanding, it should be cautioned that Piranesi and his work were in context exceedingly modern, even avant-garde, and should not be judged merely by similar but more pictorial, decorative, fashionable or strictly commercial endeavors of his day. His insights, his "truths," are in every respect as valid and concrete as the very stone caverns which fired his early imagination.

Piranesi did not concoct the 18th century passion for the antiquities of Greece and Rome himself. Palladio and Neoclassicism had already taken cultural root, the ruins of Herculaneum and Pompeii had long been under scrutiny by the time Piranesi made his pilgrimage to the Eternal City. Piranesi's hometown, Venice, was then at the height of her creative influence. The city was rich with writers and painters of Tiepolo's and Canaletto's magnitude, who had travelled extensively on Grand Tour and carried their scholarship back home with them. *Vedutti* and *capricci* were routinely completed for the edification of students and the pleasure—to say nothing of a percentage of the disposable income—of tourists. So, by the time Piranesi was escorted through legendary and already disappearing Roman treasures by scholar, builder, and mentor Giobbe, he was well-versed and poised to record his own interpretations. He was, at about this time, also acquainted with the astonishing work of Pannini, then at the height of his fame, known as, to quote Wilton-Ely, "the greatest living exponent of the Ruin Fantasy." In addition, Piranesi was introduced to many of the scholars and artists of the French Academy in Rome, from whom he gained scholarship and an even more polished technical expertise.

Consequently, fortified by a wealth of new inspiration and encouragement as well as the need to bolster his flagging financial reserves, Piranesi began to produce a series of remarkable topographical views of Rome. However, these plates, which he continued to create out of necessity throughout most of his life, were far from the mundane or pedestrian commercial ventures one might surmise from their designation. In the words of Wilton-Ely from 1988, these many well-known works of Piranesi "transformed the conventional *veduta* from a mere topographical souvenir into an image of the greatest expressive power—an image which has continued to haunt the European imagination to this day."

Nonetheless, despite the intense occupation of his topographical efforts, Piranesi was simultaneously engaged in an even more ambitious creative endeavor—the publication of his first independent series of images, the *Prima Parte*. These 12 plates and accompanying frontispiece were completed just before Piranesi was forced to return to Venice in 1744 due to lack of funds. The plates represent a collection of imaginary compositions and articulate a culminative expression of his years in Rome and Venice. His technical mastery over the demands of the etching technique and complex perspective construction is awe-inspiring enough, but it is in his wellspring of imaginative invention that the first positive proof of his genius is found. The remains of antiquity were used with these compositions as a mere jumping-off place for the creation of new ideas. These are not compositions mired in history or, worse, in the sentimentality of which much work of the Romantic era may be

Figure 7–2. *Prisoners on a Projecting Platform, (Plate X of Second Edition from the Carceri).* (CA. 1760) **Giovanni Battista Piranesi.** Engraving, sulphur tint or open bite, burnishing; Rosenwald Collection, copyright 1996 Board of Trustees, National Gallery of Art, Washington, published 1800–1809.

Despite the depiction of overpowering structural elements and apparent evidence of instruments of torture, it is the sense of atmosphere that is the real focus of this work. In addition, the human figure takes on added compositional importance which is equal to, or even symbolic of, the dissolving architectural forms.

guilty. These are essentially "modern" exercises, where the past becomes, for Piranesi, simply a "point-of-departure"—to quote Wilton-Ely. To Piranesi, the ruins of Rome were a profoundly moving and symbolic experience which, he felt, spoke to him quite literally of the tangible forces of time itself.

Yourcenar contemplates Piranesi's fixation on "irrevocable time" during this period by surmising that his interest was not so much in the facile metaphor derived from decay, reference to lost grandeur, or in the futility and instability of human endeavor. It was rather in the "meditation on the duration or the slow erosion of things; on the opaque identity of the block continuing, within the monument, its long existence of stone as *stone*." For Yourcenar, Rome's majesty did not live on for Piranesi in an "association of ideas with some buried

Figure 7–3. *Monument.* (1994) **Artist/Designer: Sergei Tchoban.** Watercolor, pen, and ink, 35.8cm x 35.8cm

Hamburg-based Tchoban is unsurpassed at the creation of deeply affecting and dramatic compositions of form and atmosphere such as this structure reminiscent of Melnikov and Russian design aesthetic from the 1920s and 30s. The hyperbolic and highly contrasting points of view successfully exploit the grand and celebratory nature of the edifice.

Caesar," but rather "in a broken vault." At heart, for Piranesi, "the edifice is sufficient unto itself." This thought is corroborated by the artist himself as he writes, "These speaking ruins have filled my spirit with images that accurate drawings, even such as those of the immortal Palladio, could never have succeeded in conveying, though I always kept them before my eyes. Therefore, having the idea of presenting to the world some of these images, but not hoping for an architect of these times who could effectively execute some of them . . . there seems to be no recourse than for me or some other modern architect to explain his ideas through his drawing . . ."

As profound an impact as Piranesi's topographical work and architectural fantasies in *Prima Parte* had affected, the apogee of his creative arc was yet to be realized. With the appearance in about 1745 of *Invenzioni Capricci di Carceri*, however, that situation would be forever altered. At once and by turns shocking, pleasing, confounding, and deeply affecting, these 16 plates with their loose representations of imaginary prisons would provide a near-infinite source of creative inspiration and fodder of intellectual debate for artists, architects, writers, and thinkers for centuries. All the conflicting elements of Piranesi's protean gifts would meld to produce a fever pitch of creativity in these works—his respect for and rejection of the past, his profound technical mastery, his precise draftsmanship illusionistic theatricality, and his Baroque theater design training. Perhaps most touchingly, they may frame a personal commentary on his ambivalence toward the human condition. In point of fact, it has often been hypothesized that an actual fever, perhaps a bout with malaria, was more than a little responsible for the febrile kineticism of this work. Actual drug usage was even suggested, for instance, in Thomas de Quincey's recollections of Coleridge's impressions of Piranesi in *Confessions of an English Opium Eater*. Still, it is as likely that the creative impulses which culminated in these disturbing images with their crashing conflicts of dark and light, unending series of ramps and stairs, and infinite perspectives were the result of a prolific creative intelligence grasping for release and expression.

Whereas, for Yourcenar, the idea which dictates Piranesi's series of plates on themes of antiquity is Time, the "hero" of his prison series is Space. In her essay, Yourcenar writes of Piranesi's series on antiquity, ". . . temples and basilicas lying open and as though turned inside out by the depredations of time and of man, so that the interior has now become a kind of exterior everywhere invaded by space like a ship by water." Conversely, Piranesi's prisons are great indomitable expanses invaded by man and substance but incapable of conquering infinite space. Furthermore, Wilton-Ely commenting on these stark economic works relates how they, "compel the spectator to undergo an optical journey of frenetic motion . . . a nervous continuum with no point of stability or rest throughout." It is true that when viewing reproductions of the *Carceri,* the eye jumps from one element to the next and while each separate component appears believable in context, they all become fantastic. In these works, the viewer embarks upon a fruitless search for resolution, but none is to be found, except perhaps for the eye's final escape deep within the image toward absolute infinity.

Panel l: Graphite pencil, 70cm x 100cm

Panel 2: Graphite pencil, 70cm x 100cm

In an attempt to comprehend these images, the actual subject matter cannot be over-looked. Why prisons? Why the inclusion of so many cables, ropes, and contraptions that can only be identified as mechanisms of torture? Representations of the human figure do occur in these works, but here, too, disorientation rather than comfort is to be found. For, when the representations of figures are not in seclusion, they appear to be nonchalantly occupied in some sort of inscrutable ritual. None appear frightened, particularly concerned by, or even cognizant of their apparent condition or fantastic locale. By contrast, most appear bored or perhaps simply resigned, and this only serves to add to the viewer's unsettled state. Piranesi himself is as impenetrable as the figures in his drawings on these topics, leaving speculation to scholars. Prisons, considered specifically, would be far less his area of concern than is their metaphoric representation. A comment on the oppressiveness of the Baroque "will to power" or a Dantesque version of the Last Judgement are two theories forwarded by Yourcenar. Per-haps these images were meant to reflect Piranesi's stance on the idea of "struggle in contain-ment." Perhaps an answer, like a visual resolution in the works themselves, was intended to be personal and elusive.

Panel 3: Graphite pencil, 70cm x 100cm

Figure 7–4. *Fonthill Analog.* (1994–1995) **Dan Willis.**

Architect, artist, and educator, Willis created this spectacular triptych over the course of many months as an investigation of and tribute to the actual building it represents—Henry Mercer's forty-four room "Fonthill" built in Doylestown, Pennsylvania, between 1908 and 1910. Mercer designed the house, "room by room, from the interior; the exterior not being considered until all rooms had been imagined . . ." A collector, Mercer fabricated much of the unique home (walls, floors, roof, even some furniture!) from site-cast concrete for protection. Willis' drawing is as unusual and organic as is its subject. It is organized, like the house, about various "spatial knots" and it rejects the usual conventions of architectural graphic depiction as far too limiting for this unusual circumstance.

Figure 7–5. *Ideal English House.* (1986) **T.W. Schaller.** Watercolor, 56cm x 66cm

A partial, more intimate view of this composition of imaginary "Lutyenesque" elements was chosen to most effectively include and involve the viewer in the spatial experience.

Not in question, however, is the degree to which these masterpieces have affected creative thought through the years. Victor Hugo, who himself coined the phrase "dark brain of Piranesi," wrote of the "horrifying Babels Piranesi dreamed of" and used them as the basis for several of his poems. Baudelaire was inspired, as were Huxley, Balzac, Poe, Proust, and legions of other writers and creative individuals. The effect of Piranesi is clearly seen in the late 18th-century French architectural visionaries. His roots took deeply in Britain and his legacy is easily seen in Soane, Gandy, and others. The post-modern movement of late 20th-century architecture must surely owe a debt to Piranesi's knowing and romantic extrapolations of antiquity. Similarly, in the world of painting, certainly the work of English/American Thomas Cole (1801–1848) must come to mind as a substantial branch of the Piranesian tree.

Cole, most commonly identified with other members of The Hudson River Valley School, diverges from his largely landscape-oriented colleagues in the recurring and abiding appearance of architectural language in his work. Rarely, however, was Cole's "architecture" of the extant, picturesque variety as seen in other Romantic-era painters. Rather, it was exemplified by more grand, visionary inventions that consistently displayed elements of symbolic and

Figure 7–6. *The Course of Empire: The Consummation of Empire.* (1835–1836) **Thomas Cole.** Oil on canvas, 130.2cm. x 190.3cm; Courtesy of collection of the New York Historical Society.

Cole's five-part secular allegorical series, *Course of Empire*, was an attempt to illustrate "the mutation of all earthly things" in a group of paintings of the same locale over time, the validity of the so-called "cyclical theory" of history, which stated that all things, all nations, pass through natural periods of growth and decay. The third painting, "Consummation," depicts an imagined society in a post-Arcadian state of wealth and power—pride before the fall.

Figure 7–7. *The Course of Empire: The Destruction of Empire.* (1836) **Thomas Cole.** Oil on canvas, 84.5cm x 160.6cm; Courtesy of collection of the New York Historical Society.

The fourth painting in Cole's series, *Destruction*, illustrates a prototypical society in a state of violent decline. While biblical reference are implicit, none is stated; thus enforces the "natural," universal aspect of the cyclical theory. This astounding image, however, quite possibly informed as well by the work of John Martin, would be unthinkable if not for the influence of Piranesi.

allegorical narrative. His "Architect's Dream" of 1840, for example, has at least as much to say about an entire society's aspirations as those of any single individual. That the individual "dreamer" pictured in the work is an architect, a "builder" of society, only makes the point more emphatic. Not to be overlooked in Cole's work too is a compelling ambiguity; bold elements of a wholly Rational and Newtonian utopia are in conflict with fragments of a more picturesque, almost wistful Romantic obsession with mortality and decline.

Piranesi's impact cannot possibly be overstated as a touchstone for the work emphasized and showcased in this book. It is especially crucial to consider his output in light of discussions of "process-oriented" pieces. For, while as stated, it can be said that all work is by definition to some degree, *process*—about something else—Piranesi is presented here as the first artist whose work is considered in a sense, *post-process*. Especially in relation to his *Carceri* series, it becomes clear that if these pieces are signposts pointing to something or somewhere beyond the page, then that something or somewhere is not materially tangible. Its goal is found, if it is to be found at all, within the artwork itself. For this reason, these pieces and many of the others considered in this and the next chapter have the capacity to approach the realm of fine art. In short, they exist in autonomy—not directly as a means of explanation about another form of endeavor. The drawings or etchings may represent buildings, but it is neither the express intention nor the *point* of these artworks that the buildings portrayed should ever exist. These pieces use architectural language not to create buildings but to create art.

"In *Carceri*," writes Wilton-Ely," we have reached a situation where each plate no longer represents but *is* an architectural experience in itself." The viewer has thus, in Wilton-Ely's view, become irrevocably involved in the creative process. So, in this work, we are no longer just a witness to process but we are the process—the process of perception. Of course, though he is unique, it is not suggested that Piranesi was or is the only architectural artist capable of this sort of artistic illumination. But an emphasis is placed upon his work as most clearly emblematic of the potential for influence and expressive power of architectural artwork as a whole.

As suggested, the Romantic Age was far from being confined to the borders of Italy. In 18th-century Europe, shockwaves of intellectual and cultural upheaval followed one another in rapid succession. Just as the Enlightenment, or the Age of Reason, rejected Neoclassicism, with its strict adherence to neoclassic and Newtonian principles as a reaction against the

Figure 7–8. *The Fall of Babylon.* (1831) **John Martin** (1789–1854). Mezzotint; Courtesy of Gavin Stamp.

It has been pointed out recently by Gavin Stamp that this artist, long known as "Mad" in architectural circles, was in fact *brother* to the notorious "Mad Martin," an individual with dangerous pyromaniacal tendencies. Still, John, a gifted artist, was at the very least "troubled" by recurring biblical visions of apocalyptic grandeur which, through all their emotional hyperbole, displayed a remarkable and forward-looking design talent. His images struck a deeply responsive public chord in his day, speaking to higher social and spiritual concerns.

Baroque Romanticism, with its interest in the irrational, emotional, and with mortality in general. Though the two disciplines shared an interest in the forms and ideas of ancient Greece and Rome, the meanings and expressions derived from Neoclassicism and Romanticism varied widely. However, both movements, with all their differences and similarities considered, were to a large extent as much movements away from something—the stifling oppressiveness of the Baroque—as they were movements toward something else. In this sense, artistic *evolution* became far more than fashion, it became a much more insidious form of social *revolution*. For Romantic writers like Goethe or artists like Piranesi, there was little shade of anachronistic sentimentality cast over their work, despite what image words like "romantic" or "antiquity" may conjure in the modern ear. To no small degree, these men and many others were pioneers, vanguards, of an unprecedented age of social, scientific, and cultural rebirth.

Not surprisingly, the French reaction to these evolutionary times differed markedly from what occured in Great Britain, Germany, or Italy, for example. In the field of architectural expression, as in that of painting where the neoclassicist David set the standard, the sobriety and reserve of that discipline held sway until quite late in the 18th century. A small group of architectural visionaries, spearheaded by Boulee and Ledoux, succeeded in advancing neoclassic style in architectural thought to its ultimate expression, and thereby achieving a new level of brilliance. "Their work is in no sense the product of the fantasies and curiosities of wayward minds," writes Jean-Claude Lemagny of Paris's Bibliothèque Nationale in his introductory notes to the catalogue for the exhibit "Visionary Architects" from 1968. Lemagny thinks their work was rather "the beginning of a great development that has reached its fulfillment in our day."

In any case, these men and their contemporaries produced a body of work at the end of 18th-century France of almost hallucinogenic power. Heralded even today for "modernity" and an anticipation of 20th-century design sensibilities, this work, which typically portrays imaginary buildings of an immense scale, combines neoclassic severity with a near-mystic Romantic surrealism. Again, the majority of these works were in no way intended for construction, but instead for exploration. These works intended to instruct, confound, delight, provoke, and inspire the viewer. Boulee, Ledoux, and their contemporaries largely rejected the ornamentation of the Baroque and the Rococo whose excesses denied the very nature of stone itself. They loved the severity of pure proportion, geometry, and the unadorned plane; they were men of Reason. Yet, to quote Lemagny, they were contemporaries of Rousseau, who "heard the music of pure proportions . . ." and "loved to give their feelings free reign. They were Romantic classicists. Their wish was to touch the soul through *'une architecture parlante'*—architecture that speaks . . . its character and function."

In one of the great testaments to both a man and his era, Etienne-Louis Boulee (1728–1799) created on paper quite possibly the supremely emblematic work of this genre—the "*Cenotaphe de Newton.*" Sir Isaac Newton, arguably more than any other individual,

Figure 7–9. *Cross-Section of Newton's Cenotaph, Interior Night Effect.* (1784) **Artist/Designer: Etienne-Louis Boullee.** Ink and wash, 39.8cm x 25.5cm; Courtesy of Bibliotheque Nationale de France, Paris.

"The shape of the sphere," wrote Boullee, "offers the largest surface to the eye, and this lends it majesty. It has the utmost simplicity because that surface is flawless and endless." Boullee's beloved perfect spherical shape was most appropriate to his homage to Newton, the "Universal Man" whom Boullee himself in the effusive dedication for this design termed the "Vast and profound genius!" and consequently he wrote, "I conceived the idea of surrounding thee with thy discovery and thus, somehow, surrounding thee with thyself."

Figure 7–10. *Cross-Section of Newton's Cenotaph, Interior Day Effect.* (1784) **Artist/Designer: Etienne–Louis Boullee.** Ink and wash, 39.8cm x 25.5cm; Courtesy of Bibliotheque Nationale de France, Paris.

At night, the interior of the sphere was to be illuminated with a large lamp to simulate daylight, while, during the day, sunlight filtering through small holes which pierced the sphere would create the effect of stars in the heavens. Newton's sarcophagus was to be the only material object in this "perfect" universe. In light of this concept's perfect realization, discussions of its "buildability" are irrelevant and superfluous.

came to represent, with ardent lucidity, the age of Reason. The principles of Newtonian physics, though later discerned to be overly simplistic in part and actually erroneous at times, formed the symbolic cornerstone of the great scientific, cultural, and intellectual behemoth which has come to be known as the Enlightenment or the Age of Reason. Science, knowledge, and rationality were, in short, felt to contain answers to any question or mystery which might come to face humanity. Schools of utopian, neoclassic thought grew up determined to reintroduce to 18th- and early 19th-century man the supposed superiority of the ancient, classical way of life coupled with then modern ideas forged by scientific discoveries—the result, a modern Arcadia. To the more contemporary minds of this post-nuclear age of course, who have come to dread as much as to praise the results of scientific discovery, it appears to be a stunningly optimistic and naive, if seductive, age.

This astounding piece, the *Cenotaph,* is overwhelmingly Newtonian in its self-contained grandiosity and is perfectly symptomatic of the age as much as it is of the man. In addition, it is a clear illustration of the effusive devotion with which Newton, often credited in his day with the discovery of nothing less than absolute truth, was routinely lavished. Though the French long held stubbornly to Cartesian universal views, when they did embrace Newton late in the 18th century, they did so with fervor. "Sublime mind! Vast and profound genius! Divine being . . ." were but a few of the epithets accorded Newton in Boulee's dedication of the images of the *Cenotaph.* The actual sphere, one of Boulee's favored shapes, was intended to create its own reverse universe within—daylight at night and night during the day. It was meant to be a self-contained and universal environment for the body, mind, and spirit—a "divine" concept to be sure.

Boulee had a successful career. He was a brilliant student and an accomplished architect, but unparalleled as a draftsman, theoretician, and teacher. Even more than actual commissions, his interest lay in his fantastic grandiose designs meant, it is clear, to carry far more weight as messengers of spiritual, social, and aesthetic concepts than as primers for actual construction. He was constantly striving in his simple combinations of pure mass to achieve what he termed the "poetry of architecture," which speaks both to the intellect and the imagination. Surely, there are echoes of Piranesi in the work of Boulee as well as precognitions of Hugh Ferriss. Graphically, Boulee's work is as lucid, direct, and vainglorious as his conceptions. The simplicity of clear, direct value readings is perfectly in keeping with the sobriety and nobility of his designs. At all costs, he avoided what he considered the *theatrical*—excessive ornamentation—in deference to the *purity* of form and mass. His crisp and economical ink and wash drawings are wholly appropriate and almost overwhelmingly effective at telling his story. Contradictorily, those stories appear to be, by modern standards, if not emotionally theatrical, then at the very least intellectually melodramatic. As a final note, the work of Boulee and his contemporaries should not be underestimated in its effect on the efforts which emerged from the École des Beaux-Arts in the mid to late 19th century.

Figure 7–11. *Inspector's House at the Source of the Loue, Chaux Project.* (1773–1779) **Artist/Designer: Claude-Nicolas Ledoux.** Engraving after Ledoux by Van Maelle and Maillet, 47cm x 28.7cm; Courtesy of Bibliotheque Nationale de France, Paris.

Possibly the most important and revolutionary of the visionary French "Romantic classicists," Ledoux designed this remarkably functional structure (for his partially realized project, the ideal town of Chaux), which typified his interest in purity of concept as expressed through purity of form.

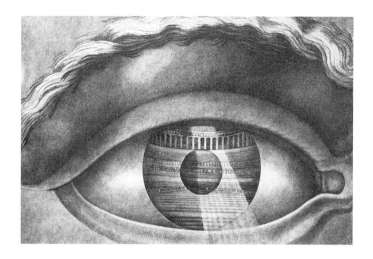

Figure 7–12. *Eye Reflecting the Theatre of Besancon.* (CA.1784) **Artist/Designer: Claude-Nicolas Ledoux.** Engraving after Ledoux, 47cm x 28.7cm; Courtesy of Bibliotheque Nationale de France, Paris.

This strange image, showing the interior of the constructed theater—one of Ledoux's own designs—reflected in an eye, is further distinguished by the addition of a mysterious ray of light emanating from above and illuminating, possibly, that which was, which is, and is yet to come.

"If you want to become an architect, begin by being a painter," wrote Claude-Nicholas Ledoux (1736-1806). A contemporary of Boulee, Ledoux was in many ways an even more self-obsessed, grandiose, and eccentric architectural visionary. He was nonetheless an extraordinarily gifted designer with a painter's sensibility for the importance of the *image*. His designs consistently employed bold and simple mass compositions characterized by surface variety, the paucity of decorative excess, and richness of expression. He shared Boulee's disdain for the Baroque and love for the "beauty of masses," but diverged from his approach in substantial ways. He was even more readily prone to self-expression as evidenced when he wrote: "rules must not impede the drive of genius;" thus he was convinced, quite utterly, that he was the greatest architect of his day. Ledoux had an abiding interest in posterity and as such, in his case, a much greater urge than his colleague to build. Despite his radical style, and possibly owing to his skills as an inveterate self-promoter, he was able to obtain a good many prestigious public and private commissions. He was a true "son of Reason" and attempted, in the words of Lemagny, to "push his thoughts to the limit as he tried to discover the prime elements of architectural beauty." He believed in the clarity and primal beauty of the circle and the square, and as such, his inventive and boldly geometric design usages of these shapes strike a peculiarly modern chord with late 20th-century viewers.

His design for an "Inspector's House at the Source of the Loue" demonstrates these sensibilities clearly. Unbuilt or unbuildable, it was an element of a hypothetical utopian city which Ledoux used either metaphorically or literally to convey his thoughts on mankind's relationship to nature and to itself. Architecture was to Ledoux the "rival of nature, out of which another nature could be formed." In this sense as well as in a similar level of skill and an unbridled egocentricity, Ledoux's path converges with another more modern visionary designer, Frank Lloyd Wright.

In Ledoux's *Eye Reflecting the Interior of the Theatre of Besancon,* we find at once a rational and a surreal image. The interior space, which reflected the image of the eye (possibly

Ledoux's own), was an actual architectural commission he had completed some time before. Perhaps the most striking element of this work is the representation of the ray of light, emanating from above and outside the space, illuminating the interior and continuing forward through the plane of the drawing and beyond. At once, in this remarkable image, we can witness the synthesis of a neoclassic reserve, a Romantic expressionism, and a touch of genius which outstrides and transcends all stylistic convention—a hint of what was, what is, and what may be yet to come.

The strange drawing of a cow's stable by Jean-Jacques LeQueu (1757-1825) is included in this discussion as emblematic of both a fascinating but conflicted personality and an era on the verge of transition, in which he labored. Unlike his more famous and successful colleagues, Boulee and Ledoux, LeQueu was haunted by eccentricities, dreams, and some say a meagre talent. Still, amply evident in his fantastic and rather florid designs were, in equal measure, the contradictory forces of the rationality of the age of Reason and the expressive musings of the Romantic period. Where Boulee could exercise his need for expression in the context of rigid design didactics and Ledoux's ego allowed him to successfully invent a unique, though scholarly, idiom of his own, LeQueu succumbed to bizarre and disturbing

Figure 7–13. *Southern View of Cow's Stable on a Cool Meadow.* (CA.1790) **Artist/Designer: Jean-Jacques LeQueu.** Watercolor, 21.2cm x 29cm; Courtesy of Bibliotheque Nationale de France, Paris.

The intellectual rigor and purity of Rationalism collides with a more emotive Romanticism in this odd but engaging work done in a world on the very threshold of change. Humor, as a tangent to extreme "reason," may very likely have been an intended component of this design for a cow stable in the shape of a cow.

expressions which betrayed a mind in torment. Nonetheless, his bold originality and inventiveness commands attention even now. One can only speculate as to whether it was humor, genius, or confusion that impelled him to produce this watercolor of a cowstable in the shape of a cow. The handles on the urn mimic the horns of the animal; this is a clue as to the apparent obtuse message embedded in this work. What could possibly be more "rational" than a building that literally speaks of its function and what more "romantic" than the desire to build such a picturesque conceit? Perhaps not incidentally, the drawing was completed in about 1790, on the eve of the French Revolution.

Figure 7–14. *Capriccio: Palladio's Design for the Rialto Bridge.* (CA. 1750) **Canaletto (Giovanni Antonio Canal, 1697–1768).** Oil on canvas, 90.2cm x 130.2cm; Courtesy of The Royal Collection, Her Majesty Queen Elizabeth II.

This wonderfully harmonius composition was, like much of Canaletto's work, commissioned by his patron Joseph Smith as an "overdoor" canvas. Unlike most of his work, however, this was an illustration of an actual, though slightly adapted, design entered many years earlier in a Venetian competition to replace the aged bridge at the Rialto. This view depicts Palladio's own design from about 1570 for a substantial stone structure (with Canaletto's addition of statuary to the roof); another architect's design, however, was awarded the commission.

CHAPTER EIGHT

Visions of Utopia

"The fate of the architect," wrote Goethe in 1808, "is the strangest of all. How often he expends his whole soul, his whole heart and passion, to produce buildings into which he himself may never enter." So much of the enduring and universally compelling nature of the practice of architecture, in its many guises, is addressed within the realm of that statement. Goethe, the Romantic, bemoans the architect's "dilemma" rather less than is deeply touched by it. He was articulating the thought, so frequently discussed in this book and elsewhere, that the *process* of creation is often, perhaps by its very nature, far more of a motivating force for the artist than is its tangible goal—the *product.*

Yet, in traditional architectural practice, perhaps more than any other art form, the fact of process is inextricable from the facts of the structure that it may or may not produce. Undeniably, much great "architecture" exists without, in point of fact, any actual resulting edifice to validate or, to the crass materialist, justify it. "In no other art," writes Harbison, "could one claim that there were two forms of architectures, plans on paper, and structures in stone and brick." We could be interested in an *unfinished*

Figure 8–1. *The Tower of Babel.* (1928) **Maurits Cornelius Escher (1898–1972).** Woodcut, 62.2cm x 38.6cm; Copyright 1996 M.C. Escher/Cordon Art-Baarn-Holland. All rights reserved.

Escher was fixated upon the idea of boundaries—"insides" and "outsides." Art and life for him were about mankind's struggle to get beyond the limits of ourselves; and to achieve the Absolute. Seen from an atypical, three-point perspective aerial point-of-view, the Tower is under construction. It is not object or goal but journey, destination, and process.

Beethoven symphony, but probably not in an *unplayed* one. Likewise, are figure sketches by Michaelangelo, for example, universally considered as compellingly equal to the completed masterpieces in paint or marble in which they were instrumental? Architecture by contrast, dependent upon viewpoint and context, does not need a building to be complete. Still, because of the relentlessly "stone-by-stone" nature of actual building construction and its necessary reliance upon, or rather, relationship to human scale, it is difficult to think of "real" architecture as being intentionally and by design fictive. Yet, it is often just that.

In *The Built, the Unbuilt and the Unbuildable*, Robert Harbison explores examples of such "architectural fictions," among them, Boullee's *Cenotaph*, the monument to Sir Isaac Newton discussed in the previous chapter. Harbison paraphrases a popular sentiment among inveterate materialists who may state that, "there are no unbuildable buildings, only unbuilt ones." While he goes on to speculate that the previous statement, even if true, might not necessarily describe a desirable condition, he also points out that, at least in the example of Boullee's design, such is surely not the case. Actual construction of the vast double dome, even if it were feasible, would dilute the purity of the concept and weaken the impact of the architecture. What Boullee has done is in perfect keeping with his "Rational" age and discipline. He has followed his aesthetic and intellectual process to its logical extreme. He has produced an Absolute, a "perfect" design, which is the aesthetic and intellectual stasis, the

Figure 8–2. *Vast Interior with Temple.* **Karl Friedrich Schinkel (1781–1841).** Pen and wash, 58.6cm x 78.98cm; Courtesy of The Minneapolis Institute of Arts.

This grandly theatrical stage setting by Schinkel, one of the great Romantic classicists, typifies the manner in which his investigative graphic work helped to inform his built designs.

"claritas" of Aquinas—pure art. His process, now complete, has resulted in a destination, in a work of art, which, in the words of Wilton-Ely, "no longer represents, but *is* an architectural experience in itself." And just as in the case of the *Carceri* images of Piranesi to which Wilton-Ely was referring, the viewer looking at Boullee's immense sphere is no longer simply a witness to process but he or she *becomes* the process, becomes the perception, not just the perceiver. Similarly, the image, as idea made manifest, no longer simply represents process but *is* process itself.

Harbison writes of Boullee's drawing of the *Cenotaph* that it has "been suggested . . . that the most refined pleasure produced by this project is the idea of the scaffolding which would be required to build it." This humorous notion only more emphatically demonstrates Boullee's aim in his work, which was (by way of an homage to Newton, the "perfect" universal man) to create the perfect containment by which the human soul could study the universe and thereby contemplate "an even greater engineering work, the heavens."

Much has been made throughout this book of process and process-oriented work. The most recent examples discussed and the focus of this final chapter are images and drawings more in the mold of Piranesi's *Carceri* and Boullee's *Cenotaph*—"perfect" or "absolute" works in which process, as said, is no longer simply represented, but achieved. These works are destinations, points of arrival, usually by design but, on occasion by pure happenstance. It

Figure 8–3. *Homeless Deconstructivism.* (1992) **Luis Blanc.** Wax pencil on vellum, 47.4cm x 38.4cm
The uncanny resemblance of so much "current architectural . . . ISM" to the slapdash shelters, devised and constructed by those truly in need of shelter, inspired this artist to lend his considerable image-making ability to an editorial and political end.

should not be assumed that by use of the word "perfect" is necessarily implying any superiority of concept or unassailability of technique or execution. While a certain level of expertise on the part of the artist is taken for granted, such works represent a full spectrum of gifts and abilities which may range, depending upon the viewer's point of reference, from the insignificant to the inspired. Strongly suggested and even encouraged by the last sentence is the development of a mature sense of subjectivity in the viewer. These are pieces that at least invite, and at best demand, interpretation. By and large, they are intended as pure ideas, as destinations, and not as blueprints, sketches, guideposts, or directionalities.

Certainly, one cannot enter, in any strictly corporeal sense, the sublime architectural concoctions represented in an example such as Piranesi's *Carceri* series. Still, one cannot help but wonder if Goethe himself would not agree that arguably they provide a far more potent artistic experience because of that fact. Within the achingly emotive framework of Romantic expression, it is the inherent incapacity of viewer and artist alike to ever unravel the inscrutable mysteries that give these works such a haunting presence. Yet, like any well-crafted mystery, there are clues and some hint of an answer within the confounding maze. In the case of these particular images, the key may be locked in the vault. Though inarguably

Figure 8–4. *Proposed Arts and Culture Center, Rome.* (1987) **T.W. Schaller.** Watercolor, 56cm x 86cm

An "ideal" object in space was the aim of this piece which silhouettes its subject by allowing it to *emit* light as much as to receive it.

architectural, how less forceful or vital would this architecture be if it were possible for it to be materialized? The real worth, the value, of artwork such as this lies in its very improbability. Like the key in the vault, its possibilities are locked within its impossible nature.

The influences of Piranesi and the Romantic Age with which he is inexorably bound were, as stated, consequential indeed. Especially in 19th-century Great Britain, the Romantic notion of the ruin, popularized by the etchings of Piranesi and others, was adapted, some say perverted, by designers and landscape architects. Mock ruins and so-called "follies" dotted the landscape and were intended to afford their owners and visitors an escape to a tangibly picturesque, bittersweet state of being. A frivolous melancholy and indulgent sense of decadence pervades many of these structures as well as the social and personal attitudes of those who built them. "The ruin taste," writes Harbison, "is an eccentric branch or twig of Rococo, which in England threatened to run away with the plant. There it remained a style with a powerful literary bias, always coming loaded with narrative." It represented, however, a taste and a sensibility which prefigured the neo-Gothic, pre-Raphaelite, and finally the Victorian era near the close of the 19th century. Ironically, these types of architecture, often

Figure 8–5. *Catskill Studio.* (1991) **Artist/Designer: Lee Dunnette.** Watercolor and pencil, 66cm x 43cm

In this superb image, the choice of color palette, handling of atmospheric effects, and language of ethereal structural materiality work in unison to convey an overpowering sense of calm and solace in keeping with the nature of a private retreat.

169

cloying design conceits, would have been largely unthinkable notions to Piranesi the designer as idiosyncratic as he may have been. Like Boullee's "perfect" abstractions, much of what Piranesi drew should, as he intended, remain on the page. When one attempts to build upon a finished concept, the effort often ends in bathos.

As an important adjunct point, Malraux points out that a masterpiece is a work of art complete unto itself. Nothing can be added, taken away, nor improved upon. In addition, he speculates that its meaning, its strength, is immutable and unaffected, as much as is possible, by context. That which is great would be considered great by any age before or since the time of its creation. However, he also reminds us that a Romanesque crucifix, for example, was not considered as sculpture or perhaps even as a work of art to citizens of the age in which it was created. That distinction was conferred only with benefit of hindsight and, not insignificantly, with the relatively modern appearance of the art museum. The point is that context and history are nearly always required for appreciation and understanding.

Sir John Soane (1753-1837) was, by 1800, among the most noted and original architects practicing in Europe. Rigorously trained in classicism, his sense of inventiveness was quickly made impatient by the constraints of that discipline. His success spanned careers as both builder and instructor at London's Royal Academy where he once warned his students of the "licentious and whimsical combinations" of a man who had "mistaken confusion for intricacy and undefined lines and forms for classical variety." He was speaking, of course, of the drawings of Piranesi. And yet it is deeply ironic, as Wilton-Ely points out, that Soane's creative focus was largely indebted to his exposure to Piranesi's works. The two met in 1778, the last year of Piranesi's life, when the youthful Soane was studying in Italy. Soane soon acquired a number of sketch drawings completed by Piranesi as studies for his well-known series of topographical views of Paestum—plates which, ironically, would go on to prove a substantial contributing factor in the development of the Greek Revival style of the 19th century.

These specific pieces formed an early cornerstone of Soane's now legendary collection of artifacts and artworks which, crammed over the years into a sort of organic museum that doubled as his Lincoln's Inn Field home in London. Drawings, paintings, and architectural fragments spilled over walls, floor, and every available surface until Soane began to literally push the physical boundaries of the house. The structure eventually consumed properties on either side and created an integrated sequence of overlapping, interlocking spaces. These rooms appear to be a living "series of Piranesian fantasies" in Wilton-Ely's words and remain today as a tangible reminder of both men and their respective eras. The house was also a work-in-progress, a laboratory, where Soane experimented, himself as guinea pig, with his architectural concepts of fragmentation and spatial dissolution. Walls appear to be free standing, ceilings appear to float on filaments of light, and in the center of the house is a great vertical space—the collection—which serves as the physical and philosophical heart of the place. Fragments of memory, history, structure, and light collide to create the most ethereal and moving tribute in three dimensions to Piranesian sensibility one could imagine. Of the house, Harbison writes, "One of the best mature fruits of the ruin craze." This three-dimensional reality and much else of Soane's best, most serious work would be unthinkable without the images of Piranesi. As too perhaps, might be the far more modern series of Best Products Stores designed by James Wines of SITE in New York. More witty and controversial to be sure, these contemporary "fantasies of decay" seem a direct, if distant, result of Piranesian concepts.

Foremost among Soane's mature and prestigious commissions was his ambitious role in reconstructing the Bank of England from 1788 to 1833. Equal to the fertile and imaginative design work of Soane, was the astounding body of graphic images created for that project and others by artist and architectural visionary Joseph Michael Gandy (1771–1843). An inordinately gifted visualist, Gandy was regularly employed by Soane in the capacity of perspectivist and, as such, produced great numbers of images of that architect's work over the years. It was a fortunate union as the strengths and sensibilities of each man meshed perfectly. Gandy's faltering design practice and subsequent financial difficulties necessitated his illustration work, and this helped, in turn, to support his production of prodigious numbers of enigmatic but undeniably inspired architectural fantasies, which he regularly exhibited at the Royal Academy.

In Gandy's bird's eye cut-away view of Soane's Bank of England, for example, we can see the artist's most mature gifts in the illustrative vein at work. Perceptive readers will no doubt

Figure 8–6. *A Bird's Eye View of the Bank of England, London, Bird's eyeview.* (1830) **Joseph Michael Gandy. Architect: Sir John Soane.** Watercolor, 72.4cm x 130cm; Courtesy of the Trustees of Sir John Soane's Museum.

The Bank of England was among Soane's finest commissions and occupied him as well as Gandy for many years. It was the genius of Gandy to complete this astounding image as if the bank were in a state of ruin; thus, succeeding in both explaining the technical aspects of structure and the circulation as well as suceeding at the more challenging feat of bathing the edifice, then nearing completion, in a "classic" light—a parallel to the Romantic views of Piranesi and Robert Adam.

Figure 8–7. *Sir John Soane, Public and Private Buildings.* (1818) **Joseph Michael Gandy.** Watercolor, 72.4cm x 129.5cm; Courtesy of the Trustees of Sir John Soane's Museum, London.

At once light-hearted and deeply reverential, this unique image provided for Gandy's patron an unparalleled homage; in a single view, his many notable commissions both completed and projected are arranged as miniatures in a vast "Soanean" space. Note again the artist's inspired manipulations of light and scale as well as the image of Soane himself working at a tiny table in the foreground.

already have identified this piece as decidedly "process-oriented," and more so if they are familiar with the project and know that this is essentially a projected view of an actual building nearing, but having not yet reached, completion. It is included in these discussions as something of an anomaly, in that it successfully transcends its use and achieves a more "absolute" state. It was intended as a formal "record" drawing of the project, faithfully and cleverly delineating the arrangement of spaces and rooms of the enormous structure. The genius of electing the patently picturesque device of relating this information in the form of a building in ruins, rather than in a more usual technical format, is what distinguishes and elevates this work. Though the structure is portrayed as being in visual decline, the implication of the work is that the bank has achieved an apriori status as a future monument, a "classic." In addition, the choice to eliminate any surrounding buildings ensures that immortal Time, the fourth dimension, is the real context of this subject supplementing the usual three employed by the perspectivist—height, width, and depth. Uncompromisingly romantic, this piece embodies the Piranesian legacy to the fullest.

Two earlier works by Gandy, *The Tomb of Merlin* and *Public and Private Buildings,* display the artist's gifts at their most evocative and theatrical. Ironically, one was a commissioned piece, a collective view of Soane buildings designed from 1780 to 1815, while the other was derived purely of the artist's own invention. If there is a message in Gandy's *Public and Private Buildings,* it is the high esteem with which Gandy regarded Soane's work and the level of intense dedication he brought to all his efforts. As a work of art, the "purity" of the drawing he completed for Soane is inescapable. This watercolor was not intended to result in anything other than perhaps the viewer's increased respect for the genius of Soane, if not for Gandy himself. It is surely a remarkable image however, as the hypothetical assemblage of architectural models is orchestrated within an enormous proto-typical "Soanean" room, to a deeply dramatic effect. Note the mysteriously intense light source necessitating differing shadow angles to be constructed on each little building. Not to be missed is the miniature characterization of Soane himself toiling away at a tiny table in the foreground. As historian Gavin Stamp has noted, this is surely "one of Gandy's finest creations and a tour de force of the perspectivist's art."

No less impressive is Gandy's *The Tomb of Merlin,* a watercolor fantasy inspired, as Gavin Stamp points out in *The Great Perspectivists,* by a passage in Sir John Harrington's translation of Ariosto's *Orlando Furioso.* A most literal reading of the lines, ". . . the very marble was so clear and bright . . . that though the Sun no light it gave . . . the tomb itself did lighten all the cave" impelled Gandy to produce this ethereal work. By the artist's own account, the architectural elements he drew upon were derived from the School of Constantinople at roughly the time of Merlin's life as it is supposed—the 6th or 7th century. Still, while historian John Summerson and others may question Gandy's scholarship on this point, few can doubt the haunting, enigmatic prose of this composition. Again in a Gandy work, we have the powerfully mysterious light, physically impossible in the days prior to electricity, and therefore all the more astonishing. Gandy's light is more than a little reminiscent of the infinite light that pierced the dark caverns of Piranesi. It reminds one too, of the light, the "spark from heaven," that so often punctuates the work of the 19th-century English writer, Matthew Arnold (1822-1888); the subject was a recurring and especially pungent Romantic theme. Finally, by way of Stamp, Summerson on Gandy is quoted: " . . . in his own particular kingdom—the kingdom of architectural fantasy—he reigns absolute . . . this local sovereignty makes Gandy, in a sense, the companion if not the peer of Wordsworth, Coleridge, and Walter Scott."

Another companion of Gandy in various sensibilities if not in fact, their lives being separated by a century, is the recently emerged figure of Achilles Rizzoli. Like Gandy, Rizzoli, who worked in San Francisco in the 1930s, dedicated copious amounts of time to the creation of his own very personal architectural fantasies. But unlike Gandy's work, Rizzoli's efforts remained entirely unknown to the public until the very recent past. In 1992, vast reserves, in fact an entire career of his sketches, notes, letters, finished drawings, and general ephemera hidden from the world, were discovered following his death, within his home. It is difficult to say what is most striking about this man, the amazing richness and unparalleled skill displayed by the work discovered, or the fact that he was not only willing but successfully able to hide it so completely in his lifetime.

By all accounts, Rizzoli was an extremely modest, quiet, and altogether unremarkable presence who shunned society and personal contact. He had a fairly undistinguished career as

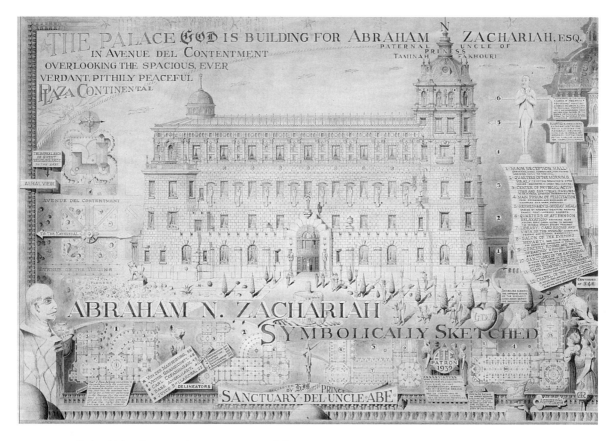

Figure 8–8. *Abraham Zachariah.* (CA. 1940) **Artist/Designer: Achilles G. Rizzoli.** Colored ink, 101cm x 140cm; Courtesy of Bonnie Grossman, The Ames Gallery, Berkeley, California.

The work of Rizzoli, who labored for years in obscurity to design an ideal city—the YTTE (Yield to Total Elation) which was to be nothing short of Heaven; that is, an actual architecture for the afterlife—redolent of Biblical imagery. This enigmatic piece is emblematic of the complexity and intensity of this prolific artist's work.

a draftsman in a local architect's office and in his spare time, of which it appears he was amply blessed, he merely set himself the Herculean task of designing Paradise. Like many artists, he was inspired by love. Unlike many, however, the object of his affection was his mother who, as rumor has it, remained within his small house for an unfortunate length of time following her demise.

Rizzoli designed the street layouts, compositions, and a great number of fantastic monuments and buildings of all sorts in his "ideal" world, which were dedicated to and quite literally planned for use in the hereafter by none other than Mom. Not yet satisfied with his tribute, Rizzoli also invented a unique language of written, if not spoken, words which he penned over every spare inch of almost every paper surface he found, including his drawings; these words are only now being deciphered.

Reactions to this admittedly bizarre and quixotic personality aside, in an objective sense, his meticulously crafted and often quite large pen and ink wash drawings are impressive in the extreme. Displaying unusual, if not wholly undisciplined design ideology, these works portray, typically in rendered elevation form, an inspired, if deeply troubled mind. Touched by mysticism, by pseudo-spiritual religiosity, and by an almost talismanic devotion to

"divine" light, Rizzoli's work is a direct and near-worthy, if essentially unstable, descendant of Gandy's. It is also striking to note that, as far as can be discerned, this is the only instance when the entire output of an artist, process and product alike, has been located intact and in one place. It is a sad but unique portrait of a unique artist.

Far less enigmatic and ethereal a figure than Rizzoli is the toweringly vital, functional, and visionary character of Frank Lloyd Wright. Though certainly, he was no less mystical or utopian in his way than his much less successful contemporary. In the context of this book, it is the dichotomy of Wright's career—almost equally divided between the built and the unbuilt—that is most intriguing. Many could convincingly argue that the only unbuilt or "paper" architecture which interested Wright was that which by sheer force of personality, intellect, or will he could bully into being. He constantly pushed, chipped away at, denied, or completely exploded accepted boundaries of fashion, of style, of behavior, of construction practice, and some would say, of taste. Still, he is among the few that can legitimately claim the title of pioneer. He went where others lacked the intellect or courage to go and, not surprisingly, the workings of his creative mind are inseparable from the movements of his pencil.

Wright, always full of contradictions, would himself deny that opinion as he routinely berated students who attempted to design "on the board." To paraphrase Wright, he claimed that "the idea must come upon you whole" and then, whatever the hour or circumstance, you must rush to the desk to record it in its purest form. Anyone who designs or draws for a living will probably be of the opinion that,

Figure 8–9. *The Chicago, Mile High Building.* (1956) **Artist/Designer: Frank Lloyd Wright.** Color pencil and gold ink on tracing paper, 61cm x 246cm; Courtesy of The Frank Lloyd Wright Archives.

Dedicated to, among others, Louis Sullivan, Elisha Otis—"Inventor of the upended street"—and John Roebling; this colossal design is one of Wright's most grand and, from a structural point of view, most sound (the "atomic powered" elevators notwithstanding), utilizing the tripod shape and tap-root foundation. As an image, it is peerless—a perfect synthesis of aspiration and possibility.

Figure 8–10. *The Odyssey Project.* (1996) **T.W. Schaller. Architects: F.L. Wright and others.** Watercolor, 117cm x 140cm; Courtesy of The Otis Elevator Company.

Science may finally be able to achieve what Wright envisioned forty years ago. With the evolution of people-moving technology, Wright's comment, "Mile high? Why stop there?" may no longer seem far-fetched. This image is as much an homage to the man and his imagination as to any tangible possibility.

for most of us, a true description of our creative processes is probably something of a compromise between these two approaches. Inspiration and investigation can be said to define creative process and most often go hand in hand. Regardless of his process, however, Wright's results are indisputable. He left behind, for a reputably difficult and visionary figure of such idiosyncrasy, an unparalleled achievement—a multitude of virtually uncompromised extant realizations of his designs as well as a staggering wealth of drawings. These images are of such individual and collective merit that, like Picasso, whatever he put his hand to has long since "turned to gold." Their nature is so stylistically individualistic that it now makes little difference that Wright, though he was an exceptional draftsman, completed very few of them himself—such was the dominant force of his vision.

Because Wright's drawings now command a sort of quasi-religious reverence, it becomes difficult for the modern architect or scholar to objectively assess their impact as pure graphic expression. Many, while having perhaps inspired someone or being at least interesting compositions, are otherwise rather undistinguished in terms of technique or media application. Clearly, it is the beauty and the clarity of conception, not the vagaries of physical inception, that establishes the enduring worth of most of these pieces. Interestingly, there exists a watercolor perspective view from the 1920s of Wright's design for the Imperial Hotel in Tokyo by that most gifted of architectural artists, Cyril Farey. Though this is truly one of the most outstanding visions from the hand of this remarkable artist, there remains something decidedly process-oriented about this piece; simply put, it is intentionally *about* process. The focus of the work, in tandem with its many other felicities, is not only the *idea* of the building but the *actual* building itself. So, despite a stellar artistic performance, it is the building itself that is the real star here. Most of the drawings—including those that may be termed less technically exemplary, which were done by Wright or his studio, by contrast with the Farey drawing—are more directly linked to pure ideas and concepts whether they portray actual buildings or not. In this sense, many of these can be seen as more "pure" artistic expressions, autonomous of the buildings they may represent.

Numerous parallels can be drawn between the 18th-century Ledoux and the very 20th-century Wright. Clearly, both were self-styled utopian visionaries with long range plans for ideal towns, which would incorporate new (designer sanctioned of course!) ways of living. They were futurists who were as deeply concerned with their own futures as with any altruistic projection. In contrast with Boullee, Piranesi, or Gandy who, on occasion, may have *wanted* to build, Wright and Ledoux *had* to. Both were deeply valid architects on paper but their dreams of immortality required more. Each had a near-mystical relationship with nature that has been characterized by intellectual contentiousness. It was a definite love/hate relationship which caused their work to, by turns, seek to dominate or to work in harmony with heaven and earth. Neither could accept the noble Piranesian notion of the fluid, cyclical, dust-to-dust nature of existence with its ultimate submission to the Infinite.

Figure 8–11. *Monument for Thelma and Louise.* (1993) **Tamotsu Yamamoto.** Watercolor, 41cm x 71.7cm

Another austere and haunting image by an artist who, with customary insight and humor, continues to question the viability of architectural "myth-making" within the larger field of "art."

Yet, it is in Wright's as well as in Ledoux's arrogant refusals to submit to the Infinte that kept their creative eyes on the clouds of future possibilities, even while their feet were planted squarely on commercial ground. Their futurist visions, even those which may have seemed unrealizable in their own lifetimes would, they had no doubt, someday be achieved by their inevitable legions of disciples and converts. Wright's proposed mile high building is just such an example. It was proposed in the mid-1950s for the city of Chicago and only, it would appear, half in jest. A supreme display of ego surrounded Wright's assertions of its structural integrity and physical viability. In his personal drawing of this behemoth, the line between fact and fiction is completely obfuscated. It is doubtful that in his heart of hearts Wright himself actually believed that such a thing could or even should be erected in his lifetime. Yet, he had disproved so many other maxims in his long career that his own sense of what was possible, let alone "proper," may have been ambiguous to say the least. What is not ambiguous, however, is the impact of this great drawing. Like fact and fiction, art and artifice become confused here; is it a dream or a possibility or both? It is, in any case, a very pure expression of a very pure idea complete unto itself. As for possibility, it may just be that *possibility* itself is the theme, the essential idea of this drawing itself that is very clearly articulated. Then again, we may still find that Wright has a few tangible surprises left for us.

In *Visionary Architecture*, Christian W. Thornsen delineates that what he has termed the myth of Babel or "the myth-forming" functions towers have served, wittingly or by chance, since Biblical times. Though historical facts are scarce, there is little dispute that sometime around the second millennium B.C. an actual edifice, a great tower, was in fact constructed in what was then the city of Babylon, near what is now Baghdad, on the banks of the Euphrates river. Biblical references to it do exist: *"Go to, let us build us a city and a tower, whose top may reach unto heaven; and let us make us a name, lest we be scattered abroad upon the face of the whole Earth" (Genesis 11.3-4).* The Bible claims its construction was to have occurred immediately after the Great Flood and the story of Noah, but in any event, it appears to have been an immense reality with a footprint of one thousand square feet. The tower also contained a central stair, that measured two hundred feet in length and thirty feet in width, and is believed to have been nearly three hundred feet in height. In shape, it assumed the form of a ziggurat, or stepped pyramid, and was constructed to honor the city god Marduk.

Babylon was a wealthy city and its legendary excess, vanity, and penchant for indulgence appears to have, as the Bible would have it, displeased God greatly. However, with the erection of this new monument, the arrogance of the citizenry of Babylon pushed a strict and apparently peevish Old Testament God too far and, in the fashion of irritable gods everywhere and without warning, dispensed big trouble. Not content with destroying the Tower of Babel, God also, in Thomsen's words, allowed "the edifice of language" to crumble as well. The survivors found they were no longer able to speak a common tongue, and so the town and the people, because of their presumption that they could rise above their humanity and become godlike, dissolved to hubris.

Over the centuries, the story of the Tower of Babel resounded in Western ears and came, with the possible help of a legacy of apparently peevish religious leaders, to symbolize the unpleasantness that we were expected to believe to occur when man dares to stand and raise his face to God's. The symbolic image of the "arrogant" tower in Europe, throughout medieval times and into the Renaissance, took on the character of visionary architecture— less a building than an idea. Consequently, only the most brazen or wealthy dared construct an edifice of more than modest height; that is to say, only towers for military defense and steeples of churches interrupted our skylines for hundreds of years.

Among other profoundly sweeping changes wrought upon the planet, beginning in the 19th-century, were staggering advancements in construction and engineering. The shift from simple wood and masonry buildings to a reliance upon iron and steel resulted in bridges and towers of all sorts that transformed the face of cities and the countryside alike. Cultural and social shifts away from agrarian to industrial-based economies augmented and accelerated the change. These 19th-century achievements were crowned by the construction of Gustave Eiffel's Tower in Paris in 1889. At 984 feet in height, it was not only a beautiful and audacious testament to the secular capacity of man, but simply the tallest thing in the world for nearly half a century.

Eiffel's triumphant achievement has never lost its beauty or fame, but in the New York City of the 1930s, it did lose its title. A passion for height as exemplified by the skyscraper seized upon the collective public imagination of America at this time. Advancements in elevator design as well as construction techniques in skeletal concrete and steel evolved from the 1880s to culminate in an unprecedented race for the clouds which would, for good or ill, inexorably alter not only the skylines of such great cities as Chicago and New York, but the very way in which humankind would forever relate to its environment. Ecclesiastical models were once and for all supplanted by models of commerce and industry as the dominant visual element of the cities and landscapes alike. Myth-making structures were now secular in the extreme and man, who had once dared to stand face to face with God, now proudly towered over Him. It is not difficult, even today, to find those who view the "city" as essentially sinful and "doomed," and the very fact of the high-rise building is sometimes evidence enough for them. The myth of Babel has been effectively preempted, assumed, and swallowed whole by the myth of the high-rise. Thomsen points out that skyscrapers have been "the dominant form of tower construction for a hundred years." Cities have long flaunted their expensive and glorious towers as arrogant symbols of pride and achievement. Around the world, to this day, municipalities regularly try to outdo one another with acts of design bravura or simple height reminiscent of the medieval "tower wars" of Pavia, Firenze, and Siena, and San Gimignana, for instance.

If there is one single figure that both represents and is in many ways personally responsible for the development of the 20th-century skyscraper myth in America, it is Hugh Ferriss (1889-1962).

It is nearly impossible, perhaps unnecessary, to separate the man from the myth he represents; he is the perfect embodiment of the ultimate symbol of skyscraper mentality—New York City in the late 1920s and early 1930s. Ferriss, like the city, was tough, proud, fast, aggressive, and, though worldly, deeply optimistic. His justifiably famous charcoal drawings of emerging and imagined architectures are unrivaled in their abilities to explain, to explore, and to inspire. He believed deeply in the power of architecture and especially in the power of its imagery to enhance and uplift human experience. There are scarcely any examples of his work which do not, on some level, virtually speak to the viewer, consoling or daring him or her to trust in the power of the future as courageously as does the artist. A complete appropriation and retelling of the myth of Babel is cast in a new, modern, and positive light, not without a spiritual element but entirely secular.

As in the legacy of Wright, it is difficult to find a separation within Ferriss' prolific body of work between the fact and the fictive. It is not that we are unaware of the differences in his drawings between images of built, unbuilt, and strictly visionary, but rather that so much of the feeling, the approach to one, is also magically evident in the other. Though Ferriss was an architect, he elected to draw, believing most deeply in the ability of the image of architecture to effect positive change in the extant face of architecture itself. A single building, or an entire city for that matter, whether built or imagined, had for Ferriss an identity, a spirit, which he believed the architect in the guise of the artist was required by faith of profession to discern and interpret. A successful drawing of a building must tell the "entire truth" about that structure which, for Ferriss, was a synthesis of objective physical realities and subjective emotional response.

Ferriss' theatrical images of utopian cityscapes resonate to this day, not only in existent structures, but proposed structures and built environments as well. Echoes of Ferriss proliferate in as far-flung and diverse personalities as Lebbeus Woods, Cesar Pelli, and Tadao Ando, in whom shades of Piranesi are also evident. Represented by the bustling technologically advanced metropolis of the future, these imagined architectures with their soaring heights, careening bridges, colliding axes, and ubiquitous notions of an alert, perpetually floodlit, and nightless society are indelibly etched into our collective unconscious. These drawings constitute supremely symbolic iconography, and with, over the years, their many extrapolations and bastard offspring, they are for us the very idea of the city. As powerfully as Ferriss moved our unconscious perceptions, he was just as busy with our conscious ones. His four-drawing series from 1922 of proposed zoning set backs for use in high-rise construction was more than just influential. It was simply adopted, part and parcel, by New York and other cities as design approach which allowed light to enter the caverns of the streets below and provide intermediate terraces above. In this respect, one may see the extent of the concession to "outdoor living" by the relentlessly urban Ferriss. He and Wright, the "organic architect," seriously parted philosophic company here.

A proposal for a habitable bridge, completed with architect Raymond Hood, is another illustration of how deeply Ferriss believed in the value of dense urbanity. While it is fascinat-

First Stage

Second Stage

Third Stage

Fourth Stage

Figure 8–12. *Zoning Envelopes.* (1925) **Artist/Designer: Hugh Ferriss.** Charcoal pencil on paper; Courtesy of The Cooper-Hewitt Museum, The Smithsonian Institution's National Museum of Design, New York.

American cities' unrelenting race for the sky was curbed a bit in 1916 by the passing of the New York Zoning Law intended to prevent city streets from becoming dark, lifeless caverns. Ferriss' rationalist response to these laws is seen in this series; beginning with a three-dimensional diagram and with considerations of structural viability, he visually "carved" away mass until left with not so much a building but the genesis of a building. One need only study forms, however, such as those of New York's Rockefeller Center to see the direct influence these "studies" had on our cityscapes.

Figure 8–13. *Bridge Habitat.* (1995) **Artist/Designer: Kevin Woest.** Pen and ink, 74cm x 144cm

The concept of a habitable bridge structure is tackled here by New York architect/artist Kevin Woest whose effort has resulted in a beautiful, well-considered, and remarkably feasible solution.

Figure 8–14. *Organic Bridge.* (1995) **Artist/Designer: Ernest Burden III.** Graphite pencil, 36cm x 49cm

The very movement implicit in the idea of a bridge itself is captured and explored in this kinetic and accomplished drawing.

ing to speculate whether Ferriss believed the "future" would be so overpopulated as to be devoid of empty space or whether he suffered from a chronic "nature phobia," he believed, in fact, that suburban sprawl would prove far more hazardous to the environment and the human condition than would a well-designed, albeit dense, city center. In the case of Ferriss' bridge proposal, one could argue that it comprises a most serious proposal and, as such, should more rightly be considered a process work, and it does point out an interesting idea—that of the habitable bridge in general. Bridges are, in most respects, process-oriented by design; they facilitate in moving goods and people from one place to another. But to think of the bridge as a destination in itself can be thought of as an intrinsically visionary concept. It forces the viewer to focus on an area we instinctually wish to transcend and allows us to "arrive" and rest intellectually in an unfamiliar region—often suspended above a great expanse of atmosphere. Whether or not Ferriss intended his specific vision of a bridge to be built is irrelevant to its impact as an independent and visionary work of art.

In Ferriss' more purely imaginative, strictly hypothetical futurisms, it is tempting to draw parallels to the *Carceri* images of that great visionary, Piranesi. There is, in fact, more than ample evidence to suggest that Ferriss was directly inspired by Piranesi. This is evident in the bold use of chiaroscuro, the dramatic compositional sense, the tension of conflicting axes, and the referential use of a variety of design elements by Ferriss. Yet, it can also be argued that the two great men diverged on many fundamentally philosophic levels. Yourcenar points out that while *time* is the primary theme of Piranesi's earlier work, it is *space* that most informs the *Carceri*. That compositions and the figures within them set their mettle against the formidable foe, but infinite Space, again and again, will not be vanquished. In more literal terms, the rather modernist shapes represented in these images—the fragments of walls, the arches, and the myriad of stairways—are at all levels, both attacked by and attacking space. Space in these works, or rather light, may be the enemy, but it is also the point, the possible salvation, and the resolution—the destiny that these masterworks address and to which the viewer has arrived. In these works we feel Piranesi's slow acceptance of or resignation to the inevitable mortality of all things—the ultimate Romantic expression.

Ferriss' drawings, on the other hand, have successfully defeated space from the outset. These soaring towers and bold, massive constructions have no fear of space and, unlike Piranesi's dissolving forms, do not hesitate to occupy that space. In their deeply secular and aggressive spiritualism, they are reminiscent of the Nietzchean "will to power." These works of Ferriss are most certainly, however, not drawings *of* space but drawings of objects choosing to dominate space. If there is a protagonist here in these works, like for Piranesi, it is light. But it is light as represented not by infinite space, but by will, self-awareness, and determination itself. These are enormously hopeful drawings. Their subject matter is revealed, always caught by surprise as it were, in an instantaneous flash of half-light of an awakening consciousness. The subject matter is at times caught almost off guard; but in these grainy and ethereal snapshots, we can see that they are more than adequately prepared to take their place both *in* and *as* the future.

Figure 8–15. *Proposal by Raymond Hood: Apartments on Bridge.* (1929) **Hugh Ferriss.** Charcoal pencil; Courtesy of Avery Architectural and Fine Arts Library, Columbia University in the City of New York.

The bridge has always been an enduring image for builders and dreamers such as Hood and Ferriss, who devised a plan to utilize the suspension cables of bridges, new and existing, as structural frameworks for housing or office space. For these men of vision, the skyscraper was but one image of the future of the American city.

Not surprisingly, it is the encroaching darkness that, if anything, threatens the stability in a Ferriss work. But the ideas of yesterday, of the past, of self-doubt, of old ways of thinking, and of being are, if not easily or completely, at least sufficiently washed away by insistent pulses and streams of light. In the process, a glimpse, just enough of what is to come, is revealed. While tension, doubt, and unease are the result of conflicts within Piranesi's *Carceri*, hope and the self-determined anticipation of resolution is the destination in Ferriss' work— the legacy of a great romantic modernist.

These images, these pure, complete ideas of Ferriss and Piranesi are not the only but rather the most emblematic of the many images in this book and elsewhere, that succeed at both illuminating the journey and the destination of architectural representation. In a very real sense, they collectively symbolize the highest achievement in the practice of architectural artwork; many have attained that state of being whereby, to paraphrase Wilton-Ely, they no longer simply *represent* architecture but have *become* architectural experiences in themselves. To an extent, any successful example of architectural graphics, in any media or level of finish, if it is lucid, cognizant of, and true to its essential idea, can attain that enviable state.

The individual architect or artist, who has reached an understanding of the autonomy as well as the inextricable duality of the object and the image of the object, is guaranteed both a fascinating journey and the promise of many remarkable destinations along the way.

SELECT BIBLIOGRAPHY

Adjmi, Morris, and Giovanni Bertolotto ed. *Aldo Rossi: Drawings and Paintings.* New York: Princeton Architectural Press in association with Studio di Architettura, 1993.

Adjmi, Morris, ed. *Aldo Rossi: Architecture 1981-1991.* New York: Princeton Architectural Press in associaton with Studio di Architettura, 1991.

Agrest, Diana I. *Architecture From Without: Theoretical Framing for a Critical Practice.* Cambridge: The MIT Press, 1991.

Arnheim, Rudolf. *The Dynamics of Architectural Form.* Berkeley, Los Angeles, London: University of California Press, 1977.

Arnheim, Rudolf. *Art and Visual Perception.* Berkeley, Los Angeles, London: University of California Press, 1974.

Baethier, Katherine and J.G. Links. *Canaletto.* New York: The Metropolitan Museum of Art, in association with Harry N. Abrams, 1989.

Beny, Roloff. *The Romance of Architecture.* New York: Harry N. Abrams, 1985.

Berger, John. *Ways of Seeing.* London: British Broadcast Company in association with Penguin Books, 1972.

Betsky, Aaron. *Violated Perfection: Architecture and the Fragmentation of the Modern.* New York: Rizzoli International Publications, 1990.

Blau, Eve, ed., and Edward Kaufman. *Architecture and its Image: Four Centuries of Architectural Presentation; works from the collection of the Canadian Centre for Architecture.* Montreal: MIT Press in association with the Centre Canadien d'Architecture, 1989.

Bloomer, Jennifer. *Architecture and the Text: The (S)Crypts of Joyce and Piranesi.* New Haven, London: Yale University Press, 1993.

Boorstein, Daniel J. *The Creators: A History of Heroes of the Imagination.* New York: Random House, 1992.

Cali, Francois. *Architecture of Truth.* New York: George Braziller, Inc., 1957.

Chang, Amos Ih Tiao. *The Tao of Architecture.* Princeton: Princeton University Press, 1956.

Cooke, Catherine and Stuart Wrede. *Architectural Drawings of the Russian Avant-Garde.* The Museum of Modern Art, 1990.

Curtis, William J.R. *Le Corbusier: Ideas and Forms.* New York: Rizzoli International Publications, 1982.

DeHaan, Hilde and Ids Haagsma. *Architects in Competition*. London: Thames and Hudson, 1988.

Denison, Cara D., Myra Nan Rosenfeld, and Stephanie Wiles. *Exploring Rome: Piranesi and His Contemporaries*. New York: The Pierpont Morgan Library; Montreal: Centre Canadien d'Architecture; London: MIT Press, 1993.

Drexler, Arthur, ed. *The Architecture of the École des Beaux-Arts*. New York: The Museum of Modern Art, 1977.

Escher, M.C. and J.L. Locher. *The World of M.C. Escher*. New York: Harry N. Abrams, Inc., 1971.

Frampton, Kenneth. *Tadao Ando*. New York: The Museum of Modern Art, 1991.

Goldberger, Paul. *The Skyscraper*. New York: Alfred A. Knopf, 1981.

Ferriss, Hugh. *The Metropolis of Tomorrow*. New York: Ives, Washburn Publishers, 1929.

Fletcher, Sir Banister. *A History of Architecture*. (19th ed.) London: The Royal Institute of British Architects in association with The University of London, 1987.

Freeberg, David. *The Power of Images: Studies in the History and Theory of Response*. Chicago: The University of Chicago Press, 1989.

Fuller, R. Buckminster. *Utopia or Oblivion: The Prospects for Humanity*. Bantam Books, 1969.

Harbison, Robert. *The Built, the Unbuilt and the Unbuildable: In Pursuit of Architectural Meaning*. Cambridge: MIT Press, 1991.

Harbison, Robert. *Eccentric Spaces. A Voyage Through Real and Imagined Worlds*. Boston: David R. Godine Publisher, 1988.

Hegel, G.W.F. *Phenomenology of Spirit*. Oxford: Clarendon Press, 1977.

Hollier, Denis. *Against Architecture: The Writings of George Bataille*. Cambridge: MIT Press, 1989.

James, Warren A. *Kohn Pedersen Fox: Architecture and Urbanism, 1986-1992*. New York: Rizzoli International Publications, 1993.

Janson, H.W. *History of Art*. (3rd ed.). New York: Harry N. Abrams, 1986.

Johnson, Robert A. *Transformation*. San Francisco: Harper, 1991.

Leich, Jean Ferriss. *Architectural Visions: The Drawings of Hugh Ferriss*. New York: Whitney Library of Design, Watson-Guptill Publications, 1980.

Lemagny, Jean-Claude. *Visionary Architects*. Houston: University of St. Thomas, 1968.

Malraux, Andre. *The Voices of Silence*. Princeton: Princeton University, 1978.

McCarthy, Mary. *The Stones of Florence*. New York: Harcourt Brace Jovanovich Publishers, 1963.

Middleton, Robin, ed. *The Beaux-Arts: and Nineteenth-Century French Architecture.* Cambridge: The MIT Press, 1982.

Norberg-Schulz, Christian. *Meaning in Western Architecture.* New York: Rizzoli International Publishers, 1980.

Palladio, Andrea. *The Four Books of Architecture.* New York: Dover Publications, 1965.

Pfeiffer, Bruce Brooks. *Frank Lloyd Wright Drawings.* New York: Harry N. Abrams in association with The Frank Lloyd Wright Foundation and the Phoenix Art Museum, 1990.

Plummer, Henry. *Poetics of Light.* Tokyo: a + u Publishing, 1987.

Powell, Helen and David Leatherbarrow. *Masterpieces of Architectural Drawing.* London: Orbis Publishing, 1982.

Rasmussen, Steen Eiler. *Experiencing Architecture.* Cambridge: MIT Press, 1959.

Riley, Terence. *Light Constuction.* New York: The Museum of Modern Art, 1995.

Riley, Terence, ed. with Peter Reed. *Frank Lloyd Wright, Architect.* New York: The Museum of Modern Art, 1994.

Robbins, Edward. *Why Architects Draw.* Cambridge and London: The MIT Press, 1994.

Robison, Andrew. *Piranesi: Early Architectural Fantasies.* Chicago: National Gallery of Art, Washington in association with The University of Chicago Press, 1986.

Ruskin, John. *The Seven Lamps of Architecture.* 1880. Reprint, New York: Dover Publications, 1989.

Secrest, Meryle. *Frank Lloyd Wright: A Biography.* New York: Alfred A. Knopf, 1993.

Schaller, Thomas W. *Architecture in Watercolor.* New York: Van Nostrand Reinhold, 1990.

Snodin, Michael. *Karl Friedrich Schinkel: A Universal Man.* New Haven and London: Yale University Press in association with The Victoria and Albert Museum, 1991.

Sprigge, T.L.S. *Theories of Existence.* New York: Penguin Books, 1984.

Stamp, Gavin. *The Great Perspectivists.* RIBA Drawing Series. New York: Rizzoli International Publications, Inc., 1982.

Stevens, Wallace. *The Collected Poems of Wallace Stevens.* New York: Alfred A. Knopf, 1987.

Stoppard, Tom. *Arcadia.* London: Faber and Faber, 1993.

Summerson, Sir John. *John Soane.* London: Academy Editions; New York: St. Martin's Press, 1983.

Tafuri, Manfredo. *The Sphere and the Labyrinth: Avant Gardes and Architecture from Piranesi to the 1970s*. Cambridge: MIT Press, 1990.

Truettner, William H., ed., and Alan Wallach. *Thomas Cole: Landscape Into History*. New Haven and London: Yale University Press in association with National Museum of American Art, The Smithsonian Institution, Washington, D.C. 1994

Vidler, Anthony. *Claude-Nicolas LeDoux*. Cambridge: MIT Press, 1990.

Wilton Ely, John. *The Mind and Art of Giovanni Battista Piranesi*. London: Thames and Hudson, 1988.

Wilton-Ely, John. *Piranesi as Architect and Designer*. New York: The Pierpont Morgan Library; New York and London: The Yale University Press, 1993.

Wright, Frank Lloyd. *A Testament*. New York: Avon Books, 1957.

Wright, Frank Lloyd. *The Future of Architecture*. Horizon Books, 1959.

Yourcenar, Marguerite. *The Dark Brain of Piranesi and Other Essays*. New York: Farrar, Straus and Giroux, Inc., 1984.

Yourcenar, Marguerite. *That Mighty Sculptor, Time*. New York: Farrar, Straus and Giroux, 1992.

INDEX